THE
PARENT
PLAYBOOK

THE PARENT PLAYBOOK

More Discussions, Fewer Arguments

DR. RUSSELL HYKEN

The Parent Playbook: *More Discussions, Fewer Arguments*

© 2012 All Rights Reserved, Russell Hyken

Cover and Interior Design: AuthorSupport.com
Cover Imagery: Thinkstock/Digital Vision/Creatas/Ablestock

ISBN: 978-0-9847032-0-3 (Hard Cover)
ISBN: 978-0-9847032-3-4 (Soft Cover)
ISBN: 978-0-9847032-1-0 (ePub)
ISBN: 978-0-9847032-2-7 (Mobi)

Printed in the United States of America

To Julie Hyken, my wife and best friend,
who tolerates my long hours and supports me
with all that I do. She is the love of my life
and a patient person.

To Court and Coop, my children,
who allow me to work in peace—most of the time.
They are great kids and an inspiration.

To Grizzly and Coco,
the family dogs, who spend hours keeping
me company while I work.

Contents

Introduction: The Parent Playbook xi

Q & A: Home Life

Questions About Maintaining The Relationship 3

   1. A Stranger In The House? 3

   2. Would You Rather Have A Discussion . . .

      Or An Argument? 8

   3. Truth Or Consequences 14

   4. Not So Funny 19

   5. Negotiating With Older Teens 24

Questions About Family Dynamics 29

   6. "Not In Front Of The Children!" 29

   7. Sibling Relationships 34

   8. Divorce And Holidays 37

   9. Different For Girls? 41

   10. Do Parents Who Worry Too Much

      Raise Anxious Children? 46

Questions About Setting Boundaries 49

   11. Good Choices, Bad Choices,

      And The Teenage Brain 49

12. How Much Computer Time Is Too Much? . . 54

13. The Great Allowance Debate 62

14. Money, Money 67

15. Strategies For A Profanity-Free Home 71

16. Too Much Texting? 77

17. Curfew Blues 81

Q & A: The World Beyond

Questions About Social Life And Recreation 87

18. Can I Change My Teen's Friends? 87

19. When Is Teen Dating Okay? 92

20. Enhancing Teen Confidence And Self-Esteem
    After A Social Setback 97

21. What Is Appropriate Teen Attire? 101

22. Taking The Right Risks 105

23. Dealing With Teen Sports Anxiety 108

24. Traveling With Teens 112

25. Can A Teen Land A Summer Job In Today's
    Tough Market? 116

Questions About School 121

26. Teens And Studying 121

27. Supporting Your Teen's Educational Success. 126

28. Dealing With Back-To-School Anxiety 129

29. Private Vs. Public School – Which Is Right For
Your Teen?. 132

30. Is Your Kid Being Bullied?. 136

31. Mean Girls. 140

32. What Test To Take?. 145

Q & A: Special Challenges

Questions About Learning Problems 151

33. Making Sense Of Learning Disabilities 151

34. When Kids Want To Quit. 156

35. Teen ADHD. 161

Questions About Compulsive Behaviors 165

36. Is Facebook Harmful To Your Teen's Health? 165

37. Teens And Obesity 171

38. Teen Gambling. 175

Questions About Serious Teen Behavior Issues 179

39. Dealing With Defiant Teens. 179

40. Dealing With Mental Health Issues 183

41. Is a Wilderness Program Right For Your Teen? 186

Epilogue: Some Final Thoughts On Parenting. 191

About The Author 195

INTRODUCTION:
The Parent Playbook

Many parenting books, and especially books about parenting teenagers, focus most of their advice and guidance on very general topics like communication, listening, and the importance of parent/child bonding. Of course, these are important subjects, but sometimes parents just want pragmatic answers to specific questions. I'm talking about questions like:

- How do I talk to my teen about a curfew?

- Should I give my teen an allowance?

- Why can't my teenage son be nice to his little brother?

- Is my teen texting too much?
- How do I regulate videogame time?

In fact, these questions are far more likely to be the driving issue that inspires a parent to seek help in the first place. What most families need, in my experience, is practical advice on handling challenging *everyday* situations.

The Parent Playbook takes an innovative approach by addressing these challenges directly. This is a collection of helpful answers to the down-to-earth problems faced by real parents of real adolescents. I have chosen a simple question/answer format that allows the book to focus on the common problems found in today's society. The big issues like listening and building trust are included in this book, but always in the context of addressing a specific parenting challenge likely to be familiar to the parents of teens.

Let's face it: All families encounter occasional

bumps and potholes on the road of life. You are likely to feel a little scared or stressed when your child first asks to take the family car out on a Friday night. Handling these situations with sensitivity can be difficult. I have written *The Parent Playbook* as a practical guide to teach families how to discuss and address "normal" stress-provoking situations. More important, this book teaches parents how to model effective communication skills—to have fewer arguments and more discussions with their kids.

You will find, between these covers, plenty of win-win solutions both parents and teens can embrace. As you make your way through the various questions, remember that holding discussions (rather than taking sides) is a life skill, one that family members of all ages need to develop. The more you practice, the easier it gets for parents and teens alike.

Q & A:
HOME LIFE

Home is where the heart is . . . and it's also where some of the trickiest interactions with our kids take place. In this part of the Playbook, you will find answers to questions about maintaining the relationship, family dynamics, and the fine art of setting—and keeping—boundaries with your teen.

HOME LIFE:
Questions About Maintaining The Relationship

---

1. A STRANGER IN THE HOUSE?

> **Question:** *My daughter is getting older, and she sometimes feels like a stranger in the house. I feel like I am losing touch with her. I know that teenagers want to be independent, but how do I stay connected with her?*

It's no joke: Teens sometimes do feel like strangers in the house. I believe that many parents who feel this way, though, are actually scared of their teens. I often hear anxious adults say things such as, "My teenager never wants to talk," and/or "My teen is rarely ever home anymore."

One of the best ways to maintain our relationships with our kids is to recognize that our own responses may be part of the problem! In this case, the belief that our teen "never wants to talk" is a myth . . . and the statement that our teen "is never home" is usually an excuse for not engaging in the first place.

Teens not only *want* to talk with their parents, they *need* to. In fact, teenagers who spend regular time with mom and dad are happier, make better life choices, and have higher grades than kids who do not. Furthermore, today's teens are more adept at communicating than previous generations were, as they are more likely to be connected to someone at home, either through technology, such as texting and Skype, or in person during time away from school. The trick for parents lies in making the effort to connect . . . And learning to make the most of the available opportunities for communication.

If talking with your teen has become a turbulent task, I suggest that you start small and simple. Focus on making "miniconnections" through eye contact and basic questions. Adapt your questions to the situation, and avoid coming across as an interrogator. For instance, if your teen has friends over, you should not only ask your own kid how her day was, but also strike up a conversation with her friends about what they're up to.

Keep the questions brief, and follow up on any initial monosyllabic retorts you receive with another question. Don't let your tone signal disapproval! A persistent, supportive parent will elicit full-sentence responses in a very short time.

Feeling more confident? Take a risk and invade your teen's space. Contrary to popular belief, a closed door does not mean "Stay out of my room." It means,

"Knock before entering." So do just that, and start the conversation by telling your teen something interesting about your own day, such as a brief story about the office or a short anecdote about the annoying guy who stole your parking space. Keep the exchange light and engage as equals. Eventually, your teen will share stories with you.

While it may be difficult for some parents to believe, most teens actually enjoy spending short snippets of time with mom and dad, especially kids who already feel connected to mom and dad. To increase the likelihood of this feeling taking root, try asking your teen, either directly or covertly, to take part in some consistent, recurring activity with you. Using food as the reason for the outing (i.e. Sunday brunch or an after-school trip to the local coffee shop) is a great way to appeal to teen sensibilities. Don't talk about tough topics unless your child suggests it. This time should be all about bonding and enjoyment.

Making opportunities to talk with your teen is worth the effort, because it will strengthen your relationship. As your teen gets closer to adulthood, you can practice things like listening more than you talk and avoiding being judgmental.

Remember: It is difficult being sandwiched between childhood and adulthood. Teens need to make their own decisions, even bad ones, but small amounts of guidance and large amounts of support will keep them moving forward in life . . .and keep them connected to you.

2. WOULD YOU RATHER HAVE A DISCUSSION . . . OR AN ARGUMENT?

Question: *What am I doing to create arguments with my teen? I don't mean to. How can I avoid conflicts that seem to come out of nowhere?*

Very often, parents find themselves in a fight with their kid without meaning to start one at all. How does this happen? Let's look for a moment at one contributing phenomenon that I call Spontaneous Problem Discussion. The well-meaning parent sees a problem and says something about it. In other words, you spontaneously ask about something that seems innocent, and you suddenly find yourself in a negative situation.

For example, consider the question, "Son, have

you started your English paper?" This may result in a variety of responses that you don't want to hear, such as "I'll get to it," or "It's not due for a few weeks," or "I'm busy right now" (where "busy" equals watching TV, playing video games, texting friends, etc.).

Many, many questions raise sensitive issues with kids today. How do we avoid conflict? We think about what we really want to discuss, and we make sure that we are assisting in problem-solving with our question . . .and not problem creation.

Let's look at another potential problem area: nagging. I like to call these sorts of conversations *psychotic parental delusions.* The truth is, we are all sometimes guilty of nagging, if not to our kids then to our spouses. My question is this: If the same request didn't work the last 22 times you asked, why would it work the 23rd time? Nagging is basically repeating the same conversation and expecting different results: psychotic parental delusion!

Most of us parents are reasonable, thinking adults, but we do this anyway. Why? Well, because it is what our parents did to us. We may not know any other way to deal with the situation, and so we act on this poorly thought-out, spontaneous plan. We nag.

Then there's the parental lecture. I like to call this "verbal brain surgery." Your son or daughter does something that annoys you, or makes what you consider a bad decision, and you think sharing parental advice based on your previous experiences will make things better.

For example, say your son's grades are slipping, and you decide to explain something he has obviously overlooked: that good grades pave the way to be admitted to a good college, and that in turn will help your son to become a success. Honestly, what do you think your child's reaction is going to be? "You are so right, Mom, I will now study many more hours. Thanks!" Boy, that would be nice, but here in the real world, you must expect a different response.

Think about it. You tell your son all about this wonderful insight that you have earned during your own life, because you are a mature adult. You send these verbal thoughts into your son's ears in the form of words, and you hope that they take root in his brain, flower, and generate new and more productive behaviors. *Has this ever actually happened when you lectured your teen?*

The best thing to do here is avoid the lecture entirely, or, if you can't do that, at least disengage when your child's nonverbal signals indicate that there is resistance. If your son is scowling or rolling his eyes, guess what! The lecture isn't having the desired effect. Your son is thinking about how annoyed he is with you—or perhaps about something entirely different.

For all of these situations, the best principle I can offer parents is this: don't argue. Ask good questions, questions that can't be answered with a simple "yes" or "no." (For example, "What kind of an assignment did that English teacher give you for your paper?")

What does arguing solve? Usually, nothing. Battle lines get drawn and combat ensues. The discussion stops being about solving problems, and starts being about who wins and who loses. Too often, it is about forcing your child to submit. Ultimately, nothing gets resolved.

To avoid this....

- *Be politely pre-emptive.* Try to make sure *ahead of time* that your child is doing what he or she is supposed to do, and has what he or she needs. Remember: The occasional derailment is okay. Be supportive when it happens.

- *Choose your discussions carefully* . . .and, when appropriate, let your child have the last word once in a while.

- Whenever possible, set an appointment to talk

about sensitive topics. Give your teen some time to get "psyched" up for the conversation. Tell your son or daughter what you want to talk about, and then say when you will ask about it. If it helps, take him to dinner to talk about the issue. Whatever you do, give your teen time to prepare for the discussion!

When it comes to teens, it is much better to have a discussion than an argument!

3. TRUTH OR CONSEQUENCES

Question: *I caught my thirteen-year-old in an obvious lie, and I think I may have overreacted. How should I have handled this?*

A recent study at Toronto University found that a fifth of all two-year-olds are able to lie, and that fully 90% of four-year-olds are capable of telling untruths. The rate of lying peaks around twelve years of age. Interestingly, the study's results also suggest that, at least as far as kids are concerned, lying is actually a healthy part of the human developmental cycle.

Telling a lie is a complex mental process that includes the ability to not only merge multiple sources of information but also manipulate that data to one's advantage. For the toddler set, lying is actually a sign of a fast-developing brain and an emerging quick wit. At this stage, the ability to lie is actually a benchmark of future life success. What's more, the ability to lie well actually indicates that a child has strong executive functioning capabilities, which are activities related to the part of the brain that controls and manages behavior. Older children who tell "good" lies are typically quite intelligent kids.

While the research supports the conclusion that lying correlates with intelligence in children, that does not, of course, mean it is a good thing from a moral standpoint. As parents, though, we should bear in mind that lying is a part of normal development. Parents should not be alarmed or angry when their child tells a falsehood. Instead, they should consider the lie an opportunity to have a teachable moment.

At one time or another, your child will lie. The best way to handle this behavior depends on the age of the child and the situation.

Preschool age kids don't always know that lying is bad and may tell a tall tale to gain interest or impress someone. Correct the untruth calmly and take the time to teach your child that lying is wrong and unacceptable.

By the time your child is at the first-grade age, he or she understands that lying is offensive but may engage in the behavior anyway. These kids may lie to avoid punishment, impress others, boost their egos, get what they want, or protect their friends. This is the time to ensure that there are age- and situation-appropriate consequences for telling a deliberate untruth.

Teenagers typically lie to avoid consequences, protect their friends, and get away with doing something you have forbidden. Before you get too worked up, however, consider that most parents will (when out of earshot of their teenager) admit that they themselves lied during their formative years. Keep a balanced approach here, and keep your cool. At this age, it is best to have a predetermined consequence for lying that is short, immediate, and painful—such as loss of game-playing privileges for a couple of days—in order to avoid an argument. You should also ask your child what he or she was thinking, not as a rhetorical question, but as a genuine request for information. Listen carefully to the answers you get, because they can provide you with important insights into the adolescent mind.

No matter the age of your child, maintain your cool and consider the following advice when dealing with mistruths, tall tales, and blatant falsehoods.

Don't play the role of an angry interrogator, especially when your child admits to the misdeed. Do, however, feel free to calmly question and discuss the situation.

If your child admits to the lie, make sure you show appreciation for the honesty. This will encourage your child to behave more honestly in the future.

If it seems appropriate, discuss how lying damages friendships. Explain to your son or daughter that if he or she can't be trusted by friends and family, it will be more difficult to gain their respect.

Avoid calling your child a liar. You don't want to label your child, and name-calling typically leads only to prolonged arguing. Talk about the act and express disappointment with it, but don't criticize the person.

Perhaps most important of all, don't model lying for your children. While you may be tempted to save money at the movies or while dining in a restaurant, misrepresenting your child's age teaches your child that lying is acceptable.

If your child lies continually despite your best efforts to follow these guidelines, it may be time to seek professional assistance. Telling untruths can be a defense mechanism a young person uses to avoid a more difficult situation or problem. As the parent, you need to find out what that problem is.

4. NOT SO FUNNY

Question: *My teenage daughter says I hurt her feelings with some of the jokes I made about her at a recent family gathering, but I say she is simply overreacting to a little good-natured kidding and a few pet names I have for her. Who's right?*

If your daughter says you hurt her feelings, your best course of action is probably to apologize. Who is a better judge of her own feelings than she is?

Many adults believe that bullies only exist at school. Unfortunately, this is not always accurate. Many kids return home to face humiliation, verbal aggression, and behaviorally manipulative parents. Then there is the subtler problem of the well-intentioned parent who "bullies" their child—by accident. This may well be what has happened here.

Of course, the intent of these parents is not to erode self-esteem, but their behavior nevertheless can have long-lasting effects on their child. Consider the parent who comes up with a supposedly "cute" pet name of endearment that focuses on a child's sensitive area by, for instance, calling an overweight child "Chunky Monkey," a small child "Shortcake", or an ADHD child "Wiggles." These names can cause deep pain and resentment, especially if they persist after a child objects.

Other parents make the mistake of thinking they are motivating their child by continually identifying the successes of another sibling. This is what I like to call the "favorite child syndrome." Mom says things such as, "If only you could do math as well as you brother," or Dad comments, "Practice more so you can make the varsity team like your sister." When a child hears these comments with regularity, he or she may begin to feel inferior, and may develop feelings of hidden resentment.

Identifying one of your offspring as more sensitive than the others can also breed resentment and sibling conflict. Suppose a parent over-focuses on one child's issues and worries too much about upsetting that child more than the others. Suppose schedules are created around the needy sibling, and suppose parents go out of their way to ensure his emotional stability. Other children, as a result, may begin to resent the situation and/or feel inferior.

Overprotective parents can be guilty of similarly misguided behaviors, and all of us run the risk of being overprotective. While it is certainly acceptable for us to safeguard our child from time to time by telling him or her, "Don't do X," we must also be careful not to overuse this approach. Continual use of the "Don't" parenting style is an adult's attempt to dictate every move a child makes. In essence, this is parenting "puppetry," and it creates only dependence, fear, and resentment.

Every parent may employ some of these misguided strategies from time to time. And you know what? That is okay, as long as we don't repeat the mistake. It's when we know for sure that something doesn't work, and we persist in the behavior anyway, that problems can arise.

To avoid these parenting pitfalls, take some time to think about how you are currently handling the moments that trigger your "autopilot" parenting responses. Is there anything you could change, simply by noticing what you are doing now by instinct... and what you could be doing differently? Here are some suggestions.

- Respect your child's wishes—whether expressed or implied—when it comes to pet names and nicknames.

- Look for ways to provide and discuss solutions, rather than ways to dictate behavior. (For instance, instead of simply telling your child to eat less, teach him or her how to cook more healthy foods and make better dietary choices.)

- Let your teen make the occasional mistake, and *then* discuss alternative approaches. Some of life's most important lessons are best learned through trial and error. That goes for both parents and kids.

- Consider that most parents who act inappropriately do so out of simple frustration. The remedy here may be the ability to take a deep breath at a critical moment. If you can learn to step back from the situation and give yourself a little time to reflect on your child's bothersome behaviors and your own responses to them, you may find it a bit easier to practice patience.

5. NEGOTIATING WITH OLDER TEENS

Question: *The other night, I got into an argument with my sixteen-year-old daughter. She was making unreasonable demands, and I just sent her to her room. Do you have any tips for handling my teenager when she is being unreasonable?*

Here's the difficult news: You may have to begin by refraining from passing judgment on what is—and isn't—unreasonable for your daughter at her current stage of life.

Think about it. Passing judgment isn't really what you want to do in this situation. When kids are little, they will usually try to do pretty much whatever is asked of them. For most kids over, say, four, and under, say, eleven, a pattern of outright refusal to do what a parent says is pretty rare. Why? Because younger kids are concerned about the possible consequences of disobeying, and because they worry about their parents' reactions if they say "No." *The teenage years, however, don't work like this.* At some point during the high school years, kids begin to strive for their independence and start practicing making their own decisions. This is entirely natural; in fact, if it *didn't* happen, that would be a cause for concern.

Inevitably, older teens begin to expect more freedom, and they begin to find ways to challenge the adults in their life. When this happens, it is time to change your approach. What once worked for you in interactions with your nine-year-old, such as repeating what you want and threatening ever-more-dire consequences, is unlikely to work now.

To help with this change, many family therapists work with parents on developing a skill we call "responsive listening." When your kids are argumentative or are just being difficult consider the following approach.

- *First, let your teenager rant and rave for a few minutes.* This is a great stress reliever that clues you into your teen's emotions; these will often be hidden in her frustrated words. When your child is ranting, that is *not* a good time to chat. Stay engaged; do not respond with anger or anything else. Simply tell your angry adolescent that when she calms down, you will be happy to discuss the situation.

- *Second, once your teen's rant has concluded, ask calmly for an explanation of her wants and feelings.* Ask what the biggest concern is. Pause, without judging your teen in any way, until you get an answer. Then, once you do . . .

- *Third, restate your teen's comments WITHOUT JUDGMENT OR COMMENTARY to prove that you really do understand what has just been said.* Postpone saying "no." Spend some time having a dignified discussion in which you show your teen how a grownup listens. The operative word here is *listen.* That's the whole reason you are restating what you've just heard. In most situations, your teen will feel much better if mom and dad will just make the effort to listen.

- *Lastly, if you do have to impose a rule or consequence for future behavior, negotiate down.* For example, if your child wants to stay out until midnight let him bargain you down to 11:00, which is what you really wanted anyway. This allows a teenager to feel like he has some control over the situation and is part of the process.

Responsive listening takes practice. It sounds much easier than it is, and anyone who has actually tried it can attest to the reality that avoiding the "heat of the moment" can be very difficult indeed. This kind of listening is, however, better than all the available alternatives for parents who are serious about learning how to negotiate effectively with their teens.

This four-step process really is an excellent, highly effective strategy, so stick with it, even if it doesn't come naturally at first. Once you master this skill, your kids will begin to understand that you can, will, and do listen during times of conflict. They, in turn, will begin to listen more effectively to you during times when you disagree, act more like adults, and make better decisions . . . which is, after all, what you really wanted.

HOME LIFE:
Questions About Family Dynamics

---

6. "NOT IN FRONT OF THE CHILDREN!"

> **Question:** *When our children were younger, my husband and I would never argue in front of them. Now that they are in high school, is it still important to hide our disagreements?*

Wow! I am impressed that you and your husband

have had that much self-control.

While I don't advocate that parents make a point of arguing in front of their adolescents, it's important to remember that dismissing or delaying disagreements can also be potentially detrimental to emotional development. In fact, it may actually be more healthy for teens to see mom and dad engage in, and resolve, the occasional dispute.

Obviously, it is never acceptable to participate in over-the-top name-calling, or the proverbial knock-down, drag-out fights. Heated discussions of appropriate intensity and length are, however, growth-promoting opportunities for parents of teens.

Kids should know that any two people who spend a significant amount of time together will eventually experience conflict. The question is not whether mom and dad disagree, but *how* they handle the disagreement. It is the way adults choose to approach their disputes that differentiates acceptable arguing from harmful hollering.

Questions About Family Dynamics

The first step is simply to be aware of what you are arguing about and where you are arguing. Yes, many teens are mature beyond their years, but certain topics should definitely be avoided. Conflicts regarding intimacy, major financial problems, addiction, or how to raise the children should only occur in private. And of course, any disputes about your child's choices or challenges should also be handled when your teen is not around. *What* parents argue about in front of a teen is almost as important as *how* they argue.

When arguments do emerge, the goal for both parties should be to model appropriate communication strategies and resolution skills. Keep voices low, as yelling escalates the situation. Demonstrate listening skills by engaging in appropriate turn-taking exchanges. Respond with clarifying statements that convey understanding. (See Question 3 for a fuller discussion of this.)

Avoid asking your son or daughter to give an

opinion. Teens will view this as a demand that they take sides; this is likely only to create internal turmoil, as they will see this as supporting one particular parent and rejecting the other.

Lastly, end your arguments properly. Keep discussions fairly short and (perhaps most important of all) resolve the conflict as a couple. Sometimes, of course, this will mean agreeing to disagree. Later on, talk to your teenager about the situation and assure him that mom and dad are still happy together, and that the occasional minor dispute is part of a healthy relationship.

Teens who see their parents engage in appropriate communication, which includes arguing, are more likely to learn how to form healthy relationships, relieve stress, and solve problems. It is the parents' job to model and teach their kids how to "let off steam" and resolve disagreements. However, if the household atmosphere is unhappy and consistently turbulent, you should seek the assistance of an outside professional. Teens who witness their parents engaging in emotionally intense, high-frequency fighting may experience depression, anxiety, and long-lasting emotional scars.

7. SIBLING RELATIONSHIPS

Question: *My fourteen-year-old son used to be best friends with his little brother. Lately, my older child seems to ignore his little brother, and they don't spend as much time together. What should I do?*

It is always upsetting for parents to see their children drift apart. Siblings share a special bond, and it brings parents much pleasure to see their kids spend quality time together. The teenage years, however, bring on behavioral changes that affect how adolescents view family, and to parents, it may feel as though these changes take place almost overnight.

All of sudden, your child prefers time with friends more than time with the family. And when he is home, he would rather spend time in his room playing on the computer and texting his friends. It seems strange and more than a little disorienting, but it is important to remember that this behavior is part of normal adolescent development.

It is important to allow your son some space to grow and encourage him to develop his own identity. Fortunately, there are still many things you can do to make sure your offspring and family still remain close. Regular sit-down dinners, for instance, are a great way to promote family ties. Cooking favorite meals and encouraging the family to eat together will help your changing child participate happily in these activities.

You can also encourage your sons to engage in their favorite activities—drop them off at the movies, send them outside to shoot baskets, or suggest they watch their favorite TV show. All of these steps will enhance their opportunities to bond.

You may also want to consider paying your older

to baby-sit your younger. This not only promotes brotherly bonding, but also develops a sense of pride and work ethic as your teen earns his own money to pay for his own things.

Lastly, don't forget about the little one. He may be mourning the loss of quality time he previously had with his brother. Take this opportunity to set up more play dates for your younger son, to enroll him in a new activity, or just to spend some quality parent/son time. Talk with him about his older sibling's changing attitude, and try to make sure that he does not take this new situation too personally. Let him know that his brother still loves him.

Despite your adolescent's desire for independence, he really does still want to spend time with his family and his little brother. As children grow, it becomes a parent's job to develop creative, positive, and flexible ideas that promote both individual growth and family togetherness.

8. DIVORCE AND HOLIDAYS

> **Question**: *I am recently divorced, with two teenage children. I've never celebrated Christmas for these kids without my husband. I am at a loss: How are split families supposed to make the holiday season special for their kids?*

Holidays can be an especially difficult time for teens with divorced parents. There are often painful reminders of the past, or new and unfamiliar routines to learn as kids spend time with a new stepfamily. Parents may also try to provide an "extra dose" of holiday cheer and family togetherness, hoping to overcome their own personal guilt. The best advice here is actually pretty simple: Don't try to relive the past or over-compensate for the present. Instead, do your best to create a stress-free holiday celebration.

Successful scheduling is the first step toward making wonderful new seasonal memories. Using a collaborative approach, discuss needs and desires with your ex-spouse and your teens. Consider what events are important, and map out their times and dates. Respect that teens may have special requests that involve both parents, such as a holiday sports tournament, or that may involve just one parent, such as a longstanding family tradition. This is not about negotiating the best deal; rather, it is about providing your kids with a joyous time of year.

These are usually tricky times for divorced families. It can be troublesome for some parents to know their teen is enjoying special moments with the other parent. Splitting an important day may make logical and logistical sense; however, a midway change in the day can be disruptive to the celebratory spirit. Both teenagers and parents may find it difficult to enjoy a special moment, knowing that in a few hours it will be time to interrupt the party and go to the other household.

Staying emotionally connected can be particularly difficult when physical proximity separates family members during the holidays. Phone calls need to be full of good wishes and supportive in nature. Consider that telling teenagers that you miss them may create guilty feelings. Instead, ask about what your kids are doing and tell them to enjoy the day. Also, make it a point to be with your own loved ones. Teens will feel better knowing you are in a good place and have the support of caring company.

Think creatively and collaboratively. Talk with your ex to avoid duplicate purchases; consider splitting high-ticket gift costs. Create a new tradition that provides for quality family time, such as a special breakfast or an afternoon of ice-skating. The big goal is to have fresh experiences so old times will not be missed as much.

THE PARENT PLAYBOOK

Many divorced parents spend hours shopping the stores and surfing the Net for the ultimate holiday surprise. The best holiday gift, however, is supportive parents who place a high priority on the emotional needs of their children. Presents become unfashionable or technologically outdated—but memories of someone who loves and supports you never go out of style.

9. DIFFERENT FOR GIRLS?

> **Question:** *I have both a teenage son and a daughter. It seems that my daughter is much more anxious than my boy. Is this because of something I did as a parent?*

This is a complex question with a complex answer. A recent study in the *Journal of the American Academy of Child & Adolescent Psychiatry* found that teenage girls are six times more likely to be anxious than boys. In addition, there is a substantial amount of research that shows women are significantly more anxious than men. If you think these findings are "sexist," please bear in mind that I am only reporting the validated information of respected professionals in my field!

Interestingly, though, our life does not start out

this way. During the infant and toddler years, boys are actually a good deal needier than girls. As kids go through childhood, both sexes appear to experience roughly equal amounts of anxiety. However, as girls become adolescents, they take the lead when it comes to exhibiting stress-related symptoms.

Let's face it: Adolescent girls face a number of complex emotional obstacles that boys do not. Their perceived positions in social hierarchies, for instance, or their reactions to the opinions of others, may trigger more intense emotional responses than those of boys. In addition, many parents tend to treat the emotional explosions of their daughters much differently than they would handle the behavioral outbursts of their boys. For example, parents coddle and empathize when girls hurt themselves, even if it is a minor cut or scrape. Boys, on the other hand, are typically told to "suck it up and move on." Parents are also more likely to accept introverted, shy, or anxious behaviors from their daughters because there is a societal perception that this is "just part of being a girl."

Unfortunately, many girls then enter high school without the needed strategies to combat anxiety now brought on by their peers. For example, when a girl has a problem, she tends to talk to her friends about it—at length. This type of "rumination" or problem-focused discussion serves only to increase stress and worry.

Girls are also far more likely to "catastrophize" their problems than boys. An argument with a female peer, for example, is often interpreted as the end of a friendship. Boys, on the other hand, will go shoot hoops or engage in some other distracting activity when they have a problem. Just as their parents taught them, they "suck it up and move on."

Unfortunately, many anxious adolescents turn into anxious adults. Here are some tips that can help you help your adolescent reduce stress.

- When your child is anxious, provide support and listen. Empathize and don't feel the need to solve the problem. This is a particularly important skill when communicating with girls.

- Encourage your teen to engage in some kind of physical activity to relieve the stress.

- Guide your adolescent to a distraction. Take up a new hobby or activity or just do something fun.

- Tell your adolescent to just breathe. Relaxation through deep breathing can actually provide instant relief from stress.

- If your child's anxiousness is long-lasting and/or occurring frequently, find professional assistance.

Your parenting style may have something to do with why your daughter is more anxious than your son. In the bigger picture, however, other influences may have more to do with this condition. Either way, it is good to recognize that each of your teenagers is different and provide each with the support they need to be successful.

10. DO PARENTS WHO WORRY TOO MUCH RAISE ANXIOUS CHILDREN?

> **Question:** *My husband says that I worry so much about the outside world that our house is no fun for our teens. He also says I'm giving them a complex. I think he's overreacting, because all I'm really doing is thinking ahead and showing concern. Who's right?*

Anxiety may be biological, but we have the power to control both parental and child anxiety . . . because we can create an environment that allows us to do so.

Today's children and parents have a lot to be anxious about, and teens now face concerns that are much bigger than the classic "monster under the bed." There is 24/7 news coverage that tells about tragic, hostile, and scary situations from all around the world. There are Internet predators, chemicals in our food, real-life predators, medical vaccination concerns, high divorce rates, and on and on. No place is safe. Tragedies can happen at school, at the mall, and at the neighbor's house down the street.

It is natural for parents to worry about problems their teens could face, but too much worry will have a negative impact on your children's development. Overly anxious parents tend to be critical and catastrophizing—meaning they routinely look for new problems, then emphasize and exaggerate their potential risks. If this is what is happening in your home, then I'm afraid your husband may be right. Habitual worst-case-scenario worrying creates a home where kids, too, become worriers. If you don't want to raise anxious children, then you need to provide an environment that will help your kids reduce the impact of life's stressors.

THE PARENT PLAYBOOK

Here are a few tips:

- *Control the need to control.* As parents, you really can't control what your teens or their friends do. You can, however, control your thoughts, feelings, and reactions, and you can teach your child to do the same.

- *Plan.* Planning reduces anxiety, and worrying is not an effective way to deal with a situation. Teach your kids to plan effectively as a response to stress, and both you and your children will worry less.

- *Relax.* Everyone should know a few relaxation techniques. Breathing, listening to music, or gentle stretching can turn a tense situation into a doable task. Practice a few relaxation techniques until you find that they work for you, and then show your children how to use them.

HOME LIFE:
Questions About Setting Boundaries

---

11. GOOD CHOICES, BAD CHOICES, AND THE TEENAGE BRAIN

Question: *Sometimes it seems like my teenager has forgotten how to use her brain . . . and she makes really poor decisions. She knows what is right but too often chooses to do what is wrong. Why is this?*

Adolescence is the second (and, to parents, more surprising) stage of life when we act like little kids.

Don't be surprised if your teenager throws tantrums and makes unreasonable demands that one might typically associate with the terrible twos. Together, you have just entered the "terrible teen" zone, and it's not a lot of fun for either side.

Here is the thing to remember: Most teens actually know when their behavior is inappropriate. In fact, if you ask teens whether drinking and driving is dangerous, or whether eating an entire pack of Oreos is unhealthy, or whether they should pick their dirty laundry up from the floor and put it in the washing machine once in a while, they will give you all the right answers! So . . . why do they pretend to be asleep when it is time to do household chores? Blame it on the brain!

Teens are people with extremely sharp minds who just are not yet sure what to do with them. For instance: Adults understand risk at a very high level, because our brains are fully developed, and because we've had a lot of practice using those brains to deal with risk. Teens, however, don't organize and understand life in the same manner that we do. A full-grown body does *not* equal a full-grown brain!

During adolescence, the teen brain is only about 80% developed; it does not mature until the middle twenties. Because teens' brains are still growing, environmental factors can significantly affect their developing minds.

Teenagers are truly information sponges; adolescents are more capable of learning, memorizing, and retaining information than most adults. So why do these highly intelligent beings sometimes do stupid things? Because impulse trumps logic!

Just as the brain allows teens to learn and retain information, it also makes adolescents susceptible to negative influences. Primal instincts can take over, causing teens to choose what feels good over what is right. In fact, there is a specific part of the brain, the amygdala, that *causes* kids to follow these urges, rather than following their intelligence. For these teens, feeling good really is more important than making good decisions; for these teens, watching television really is more important than studying for a test.

To avoid negative brain development, parents should monitor their child's activities and encourage her to use her brain productively. As teens grow, the brain starts to prune away the unused portions and hardwire the most-used areas. This means that kids who are involved in academics, sports, music, and similar activities will hardwire their brains to better absorb and enjoy these activities. Kids who are allowed to be lazy, on the other hand, will hardwire their brains to be adult couch potatoes!

Positive support for your adolescent is the best way to ensure proper brain development. Teenagers need to be surrounded by compassionate adults and caring institutions that help them learn specific, consistent, and appropriate behaviors. This does not mean you should forgo discipline when teens make poor, impulsive decisions, but it does mean you should make a point of talking about how your teen is feeling right now . . . and how he or she would have felt after doing the "right thing."

As you pose these kinds of questions, make sure you are coming across as supportive, rather than as a lecturer. Remember, your goal here is to have a discussion, not an argument! (See Question 2.)

12. HOW MUCH COMPUTER TIME IS TOO MUCH?

Question: *My mind reels when I think about how much time my son spends playing videogames, texting people, and visiting websites. The whole online thing feels like it's getting out of hand. What do I do?*

According to the American Medical Association, approximately 90% of American youth enjoy videogames. Somewhere between 8.5 and 15% of those gamers play so excessively that they are addicted.

The term addict used to be reserved for individuals involved with drugs and alcohol, but videogames have redefined the word in recent years. Addiction now refers to any situation initially thought to be pleasurable but over a period of time becomes needed in order for us to feel "normal."

Thus, addiction no longer refers only to physical substances like drugs and alcohol; the medical profession now recognizes that a wide variety of substances and activities can cause someone to become compulsively dependent.

Videogames are literally *designed* to be addictive. Great graphics, sensational and/or titillating themes, realistic characters, and just the right amount of challenge often makes interacting with computers feel more rewarding than spending time with friends. The addiction starts with the quest to post a high score, the desire not only to beat others, but also set a personal best. This often causes players to seek out online communities where "the game" is the common social thread. Cyber relationships are formed, and the compulsion to play and interact on the Internet replaces the desire for face-to-face contact.

The symptoms of videogame addiction are obvious, but many parents choose to overlook them because the kids are at home and the dangers of the "outside" world remain outside. Unfortunately, this justification can impede your teen's social, interpersonal, and mental development. Parents need to understand and take action on the warning signs of videogame addiction!

The first and most obvious indicator is that your teen spends most of his waking hours in front of a screen. This leads to things like falling asleep at school, cutting corners on or overlooking schoolwork (and the slumping grades that result), and dropping out of social activities. Some kids may lie about how much time they spend online and may become irritable when their fingers are not around a game controller. Physical signs such as carpal tunnel syndrome, backaches, and dry eyes may also be present.

It is natural for kids and parents to argue about what

constitutes appropriate computer use, but even if a teen gives "pushback," parents need to engage, set ground rules and then *stick to the plan* to help kids avoid addiction.

With that in mind, you should, at a minimum, take the following steps sooner rather than later.

- *Mandate time away from the computer.* Don't just limit game time, set parameters around all screen time.

- *Predetermine the consequences of breaking the family rules about computer use.* This will help you to avoid arguments when rules are violated. It's out of your hands!

- *Keep videogames and computers out of the bedroom.* Place the computer in an area where you are likely to walk in at any moment. Then *make a habit of walking in at any moment!* This helps you help your teen avoid late night playtime and minimizes the likelihood of "sneaky" access.

- *Set up a central charging station* (again, far from bedrooms) where you can plug in all video-capable electronic devices, such as cell phones, for the night. This also prevents late night use.

- *Turn off* cell phones, TVs, and other communication devices during meal times.

- *Insist your children participate in at least one weekly "extracurricular" activity where mobile devices can't be used.* Football, ballet, or bowling, for example.

- *Have all family members (including adults) turn off the technology* after a specified time each night. This is an area where you must lead by example!

- *Physically take the games away for an appropriate amount of time.* This is something you must be willing to do if your kids simply refuse to take a break!

- *Seek professional help* if the problem persists and causes undue stress.

- *Stick with your household rules!* When your kids say they have nothing else to do but play videogames, challenge them to a game of basketball, pull out a deck of playing cards or, if all else fails, remind them there are always household chores to be done.

A recent survey reports that kids now spend more time listening to music, playing games, and watching TV on their cell phones than talking on them. Even more surprising is that most of the students surveyed commented that their parents *do not have rules in place* about how much time they can spend watching TV, playing videogames, or surfing the net. This, in my view, is a recipe for disaster.

I recently read an article on WebMD that discussed Internet addiction. Researchers examined the relationship between psychiatric symptoms and Internet addiction in 2,162 junior high students over a period of two years. About 11% of study participants were classified as having an Internet addiction in the initial assessment. That is an alarmingly high statistic!

The Internet can be, and all too often is, used in an unhealthy way as an escape from reality. In a world where kids often feel powerless, cyberspace is a place where they can feel in control . . . but this feeling comes at the unacceptably high cost of losing control of one's relationships, one's ability to learn, grow, and contribute, and one's sense of self. Just as an addict takes drugs or alcohol to mask personal pain or escape reality, teens (and adults!) may hide in the electronic world to avoid real life.

Watch your kids to see if the amount of time on the Internet is excessive. Does your Internet addict forgo other pleasurable opportunities to engage electronically? Is he unpleasant when not engaged with a game controller? A temporary obsession might be developmentally appropriate, especially if there is a newfound game or website . . . but a recurring pattern of long hours spent in front of a screen might be a sign of addiction.

Many teens can find the balance between connecting online and connecting in person; however, parents should not assume that that balance is in place. One good way to do this is to take advantage of the fact that teenagers will always understand computers much better than any adult. Today's kids don't "go" online . . .. unless we intervene, they ARE online 24/7, because technology is part of their everyday lives!

Consider reversing the roles a bit and asking your teenager to spend some time with you . . . so he or she can show you how to use the latest technologies. This is a great way to connect with your kids, learn something new, and put the emphasis back on person-to-person interactions in your family.

13. THE GREAT ALLOWANCE DEBATE

Question: *In the past, I have always just given my kids money. Now that my son is older, should I provide him with a "no strings attached" allowance, or make him work for the cash?*

Typically, kids are more than willing to spend money freely... as long as it comes from their parents. Some kind of weekly allowance arrangement can be an excellent way to teach your teen the value of a dollar, especially if you provide the proper support in learning about money management. But what kind of allowance should it be?

Once a parent commits to the "give the kid some money" process, a dilemma faced by every parenting generation quickly presents itself. Should you just hand over a certain amount of cash each week to your excited teen, or should you require chores before shelling out the bucks? Both approaches have their advantages.

Flat allowances emphasize the importance of the family unit, and help send the message that all members take care of each other, no matter what. Chore-based allowances teach teenagers the relationship of work to money and foster a strong work ethic, as kids earn for doing. There is no one correct answer, and each family must make this important decision based on its own unique situation. While most parents are quick to teach their kids about good hygiene, good manners, and good nutritional habits, they often overlook the importance of fiscal responsibility. Be consistent and clear about money expectations, talk about money constructively together, and you will raise a child who understands the value of a dollar, regardless of the decisions you make about the structure of the arrangement.

However, you should make sure your decision is an informed one, and you should make an effort to execute that decision in support of your child's financial learning process. A flat allowance, for instance, does not mean that your son should do nothing. In fact, it means just the opposite! All children in every family should be required to have specific responsibilities with specific consequences. These tasks, however, should not, in my view, be tied to getting paid; rather, they should be tied to a specific privilege or consequence (such as loss of "screen time" for gameplay and entertainment). The goal of the "consistent cash" approach is to teach kids how to manage money, not to win behavioral leverage. Using a withheld allowance as punishment may well deprive your child of valuable life lessons.

One of the most positive aspects to providing a

modest weekly stipend is that your son will quickly learn that what Mom and Dad provide does not come close to covering all the costs of all the stuff he wants. By offering additional money-making opportunities, you can help your son see that hard work has its rewards. Furthermore, reaching a specific monetary goal and buying the prized possession instills a sense of pride that many people remember for decades.

You should probably also consider making older adolescents personally responsible for bigger-budget items, such as clothes and a cell phone. Whichever path you choose, you should clarify your spending expectations and have regular discussions about money management to ensure understanding and compliance. Don't be afraid to let your teen make a few bad financial decisions along the way. After all, it is better to make a fifty-dollar mistake at age 15 than a five-thousand-dollar mistake at age 25.

This is your decision as a parent, and you should

make it after due consideration of the financial and emotional realities your family faces. The only truly wrong answer is to rob your son of the opportunity to learn valuable life lessons about money and work... by simply giving him cash whenever he asks for it.

14. MONEY, MONEY

> **Question:** *My teenager constantly asks us to buy expensive things for her and says she will pay us back. The problem is, she rarely does. How should we react to her requests?*

Does your daughter understand interest rates, know that ATMs charge fees, or have the skill to balance a check book? If not, it's time for her to find out.

Did you know that almost a third of all teens have some form of personal debt (Source: Schwab, 2007 Survey)? Teens are intelligent, but they still need mom and dad to help guide them toward fiscal responsibility.

Most cash conflicts with teens occur as impulsive adolescents struggle to learn the difference between wants and needs. They often cajole their parents for money to buy some "must-have" item or other. Don't automatically give into their pleas; take this opportunity to find creative ways to educate and inform your brand-seeking offspring about the value of a dollar.

Start by discussing cash-saving strategies. Teens can acquire money through jobs, allowances, and gifts. Your daughter should develop a "pay myself first" attitude by placing a predetermined amount of her income into a special account. This habit will help her to understand that spending is part of earning . . . but it should typically take place only after saving has occurred.

Defining financial objectives is another essential component of teaching money management. Discuss long/term needs (like a college education) and compare them with short term wants (like the latest videogame). Set goals for both but make sure you start by saving small, tangible amounts that will allow your daughter to experience some short term success. It is easier to save five dollars per week than fifty dollars per month.

Parents should also share real-life financial lessons by including their teens in occasional discussions about household budgeting and bill paying. Most kids do not know about utility bills or understand how much money it takes to feed a family. Exposing them to these expenses will not only educate your teens about the process of financial management, but may also result in a better sense of how much the things that your teens take for granted really cost.

Lastly, teach your teen to manage her own money. Give her a budget to cover living expenses such as food, clothing, and gas. Celebrate her successes, but allow her to feel the pain of a poor purchase decision. Overspending on a fancy new pair of shoes may mean that she does not have enough money to go to the movies! Who knew?

Remember, as teens enter college, they become

eligible for credit cards, loans, and other payment plans. Life lessons in money management may have to be learned the hard way if your teen does not learn how to manage her spending while she is still living at home.

15. STRATEGIES FOR A PROFANITY-FREE HOME

Question: *Our two kids—a boy, sixteen, and a girl, fifteen—have begun using rough language around the house, language that we really don't approve of. What can we do?*

I can still remember the first time I heard my own child use a swear word. He had no idea what it meant, and the context was so funny that I laughed out loud. Seeing my reaction, my son, who was just three years old at the time, decided not just to say the word again, but to sing it at the top of his lungs. Once I pulled my composure together, my parenting sense kicked in, and I told him purposefully that he was not to use that word again. I was drawing a line, one that we ended up defending successfully in our family.

Unfortunately, cursing is becoming more commonplace in all corners of our society. A recent survey commissioned by Care.com found that 86% of parents believe that the current generation of children is cursing more and using inappropriate language at an earlier age than those parents did when they were kids.

Why do kids curse? For younger children, as my own experience with my son suggests, inadvertent cursing is just a natural part of language learning. They don't understand the concept of "taboo" words, but simply mimic speech and phrases that they hear. As children get older, they hear this language at the playground, on cable television, in their music, and at the movies. Due to peer pressure, a desire to impress their friends, or the goal of being part of the group, these inappropriate sayings start getting more and more use.

Parents need to take control of this situation. Different ages, however, deserve different rules and explanations. Typically, until around age six, kids should simply be told not to use those words, and that they are bad. No further clarification is needed. As kids get older and can understand more abstract concepts, deeper explanations are warranted. This often means defining the words in question, since these kids often have no idea what they are actually saying, and then have a serious talk about the best ways to express feelings appropriately.

As kids enter the teen years, which in many families is when cursing peaks, the parenting goal changes. Now, the goal is to draw appropriate boundaries. Teens will use profanity around their peers, and there is really nothing a parent can do about this except monitor the situation and set some ground rules for behavior that affects others. Learning to negotiate and follow such ground rules is, of course, an important part of becoming an adult.

Adolescents should never curse at school, around adults, or in public, no matter how angst-ridden they may be at any given moment. Parents need to set and calmly defend this boundary. Another boundary is just as important, but perhaps more difficult to defend: Bad language, when it does occur, should be an expression of frustration or an "intensifying" adjective; it should not be part of a mean, angry attack on a peer. If profane rants that are meant to hurt other people occur frequently, around peers or anyone else, parents need to understand that this is not only unacceptable, but also a sign of a possible bigger problem.

Last but certainly not least, parents need to set the example themselves . . . and stop cursing.

Below are strategies, some adapted from the excellent web site Care.com, that can help you to make your household profanity-free.

- *Just say no.* Tell your children that curse words are not acceptable in your home. Consider brainstorming some more acceptable words that can be used instead.

- *Be honest and admit it when you mess up.* If your child hears you curse and calls you out, explain that you, too, struggle with this issue. Thank your child for reminding you. This will have the added bonus of making your child feel like he or she is facing an adult problem.

- *Create consequences.* Add a chore around the house or take away screen time every time your child curses in front of you. Tell your child about the consequences up-front so he or she knows what to expect.

- *Use the Swear Jar.* Create a financial penalty for the use of profanity. In many families, parents put *way* more money into the jar than the kids do! Use the cash for a fun family activity.

- *Correct houseguests.* If you hear a guest in your home swear, politely ask the guest not to use those words. If the guest persists, pull him or her aside and calmly explain that you are trying to teach your children that those words are not acceptable.

- *Choose TV and movies carefully.* For family viewing time, pick movies in which language is not going be a problem. There are plenty of parent-friendly online reviews that will help you to pick the right entertainment. Remember: Even when you think your children are not paying attention to bad language in a film . . . they probably are.

16. TOO MUCH TEXTING?

> **Question**: On my most recent cell phone bill, I noticed that my teenage son had 1500 text messages. Doesn't this seem like way too much?

"OMG!"

That's text talk for "Oh my God," and I'm suspecting it's a good approximation of how you felt when you saw the bill. It's true that 1500 messages sounds like a lot, but (assuming you have the right calling plan) it may not be. That's because today's teen texts for a variety of reasons. How, why, and when your son communicates may be more important than the actual number.

Technology has changed the way modern-day kids communicate. Remember that our generation spent hours gossiping on the phone; today's teen often chooses to engage with peers electronically, through text messaging. Balancing the demands of after-school activities, jobs, and homework can be complicated. Mobile communication helps kids keep on top of everything and stay connected to one another, too. In fact, many students actually define their social circles through broadband bonding.

The good news is that parents can participate, too. Digital devices are getting smaller and cheaper. Parents should embrace these advances because texting offers an easy way to stay discreetly connected with your teen. Since friends won't know that your son is communicating with Mom or Dad, he is actually more likely to keep you informed of his activities and whereabouts. Texting sometimes offers the added bonus of attitude-free communication, because you won't hear the "tone" of your teen's voice when he replies. Talk about a win-win!

Questions About Setting Boundaries

Managing your teen's cellular use is an excellent way to promote fiscal responsibility. Speak to your son about the cost of telephone technology and take a trip to the phone store. Would your son rather have more talk minutes or more text messages? Does he plan on downloading music or sending photos? Evaluate the different packages and work together to decide what is most important, what is unnecessary, and which plan is most affordable. Agree on how much your child will pay and the due date of his payment to you.

Cell phones may seem like a necessity these days, but they are also a privilege. Develop specific guidelines on acceptable cell phone use. Emphasize the importance of face-to-face communication, and require your son to put the phone away during family meal times. Some teens will want to text into the late hours of the night; negotiate a phone curfew. Set up a charging area and require teens to put the phone away and "plug in" by a certain time.

I encourage today's parents to learn how to text safely—as in, not while driving. This will keep you connected with your teen even when he is far away. Your son will smile when he gets a "good luck" message before the big game. Teach your spouse to text, and *you* will be able to smile when sending a message to pick up dinner on the way home!

17. CURFEW BLUES

> **Question:** My son and I have been arguing about his curfew all summer. We have different opinions about what it should be. This has also created a problem for his younger brother, as he feels that his curfew should be the same. How do you determine what is an appropriate time?

Curfew controversies have been a source of contention between teens and parents for many generations. We argued with our parents about it, and now we are faced with the same situation.

Parents are likely to view curfew issues as security and safety questions, particularly with headlines that warn them about late night parties that get out of hand, drug and alcohol abuse, drunk drivers, and various kinds of predatory adults. Unfortunately, most adolescents feel that curfew rules are little more than a parental power play, and are more concerned about their own freedom and independence than about parental feelings and concerns. This situation, however, is an opportunity to teach your kids about setting limits, social responsibility, and common courtesy. It is an important conversation, so prepare for it wisely.

Set up a family meeting to discuss nighttime boundaries. Before that meeting begins, check the local laws in your community and ask other parents what limits they have set.

During the meeting, ask your teens to share their ideas and insights about curfew *before* you attempt to "lay down the law." Listen to what they have to say. Reach an agreement on curfew time *together;* this will provide the best opportunity for success.

Once you have established the curfew, determine the consequences with your teens' assistance. There is typically very little arguing when enacting jointly created, predetermined rules during your family meeting. Attempting to enforce a consequence "on the spot"— i.e., right after your child has violated the rules— could result in a volatile exchange, and perhaps in an emotionally-driven decision that you will regret.

The whole reason for imposing a curfew is parental concern, and your children should know this. During the family meeting, explain that you trust them to make good decisions, but you are concerned about their safety and about what impact the behavior of others may have on their lives. Once your teens get a sense for your personal concern, they are more likely to think of getting home on time as a simple courtesy that allows mom and dad to sleep more and worry less.

Post the rules on the refrigerator for all to see and provide the occasional reminder to ensure your child's compliance. Say things like "See you before midnight" as they are walking out the door. Make sure these are gentle reminders about curfew times; your tone should not provoke arguments.

If your teen is late, *make sure you ask why* before implementing the punishment. On occasion, there may actually be a good reason for the momentary lapse of responsibility. If there is, be sure to take advantage of this chance to connect and discuss bigger issues.

One final word of advice about curfews: Don't be too rigid. As your teens become more responsible, tell them how much you trust them, and begin to ease up on the rules. This will foster open and honest parent/teenager communication . . . and allow you to stay involved in the lives of your kids.

Q & A:
THE WORLD
BEYOND

It's sometimes hard for parents to remember, but growing up is all about learning more about the outside world, finding a place in it, and establishing confidence and independence outside the home. In this part of the Playbook, you get answers to some of the most important questions about teen life beyond the family environment.

THE WORLD BEYOND:

Questions About Social Life And Recreation

---

18. CAN I CHANGE MY TEEN'S FRIENDS?

> **Question:** *I don't like my daughter's friend. Should I try to forbid her from spending time with this friend?*

What most parents do not realize is that their intelligent teens know quite well when mom or dad disapproves of a friend. Your daughter does care what you think, but she will often ignore your feelings in pursuit of her independence. This leaves you wondering why in the world your intelligent child would choose to spend time with "that kid."

Here's the part parents often don't take into account: during the teen years, most kids are searching for their identity by trying on different roles. They experiment with appearance, by spending time with a new peer group, and by continually altering and updating their attitudes. The process can be quite confusing for the parent, but it is all part of the developmental process.

Whenever a parent does not like a new-found friend, I suggest that the most important thing to do first is to *reflect upon your own reasoning* and then do something about it. Ask yourself whether you have gotten to know the object of your angst. Have your daughter invite the friend over and engage in some light conversation. Discuss school, personal interests, and family history. Don't hover, but do offer to rent them a movie or make them lunch.

At this point, you can encourage your daughter to spend time socializing at home with all of her friends, even the friends you do not like. When she is at someone else's home, contact the other teen's parents and ask about household rules, curfews, and supervision. These strategies will help alleviate your anxieties, and also help you to gain insight into how your daughter forms peer relationships.

Unfortunately, despite your best attempts, you may find that you truly don't like the friend's personality. At this point, I'm afraid my advice is difficult for a lot of parents to follow: Get over it. It is acceptable to politely discuss qualities that offend, or specific behaviors of the friend that concern you, but it is a waste of time to criticize your daughter's choices. Negative comments from you will inadvertently insult her intelligence and drive her toward, not away from, the intolerable companion. Further, she will very likely attempt to justify the relationship, resulting in a parent/teen showdown.

Now, it is possible, of course, that the friend is truly bad news. When your parental intuition tells you that your daughter's friend will influence her in a harmful and destructive manner, it is time to intervene. Highlight the behaviors that trouble you and ask your daughter how she will avoid making poor decisions. Assist your teen to develop decision-making muscles and evade the influences of negative peer pressures.

These situations may rise to a level of significant tension in your mother/daughter relationship. If things get really rocky, don't disengage from your teen; rather, foster communication with the assistance of a mental health professional. A good counselor can help present differing perspectives and encourage understanding from both sides.

Questions About Social Life And Recreation

Note: If you're reading this, and congratulating yourself that this problem hasn't yet presented itself in your home, don't worry. It will. Your teenager will eventually find a new friend who leaves you scratching your head in disbelief. This parental rite of passage is just one more bump in the road, one more way of earning your "parenting stripes." As long as your teen is responsible and respectful, it is her right to choose who is worthy of her free time.

19. WHEN IS TEEN DATING OKAY?

Question: *Last month, my ninth-grade son asked me to help him pick out a Valentine's Day present for his girlfriend. He seems so young to have a girlfriend. What age is normal for kids to start having dates?*

First, you should realize that it is great that your son still wants his mother's input. When kids enter high school, they often start relying on their friends more than their parents. I hope you were able to help your son, and that he had a positive experience with you during what may be a difficult time.

There are no hard and fast rules about the age at which dating should start. Even so, I have outlined the stages of what I call "dating development." These may provide insight into your question and help your child negotiate early romantic encounters.

- *Stage One: Since I love you, I am going to call you names.* Believe it or not, most of us become attracted to the opposite sex at about the age of ten or eleven; we just don't know what to do. First crushes form but many try to keep their "dreamboats" a secret to avoid embarrassment. Sometimes, we are even mean to the objects of our desire to hide our true feelings. Kids are usually too young to understand romance and, as a result, crushes are often not returned. Bottom line: This is a pretty confusing time.

- *Stage Two: I like you, but do you like me?* Things get a little better around age twelve or thirteen. We are still too young to truly understand romance, but members of the opposite sex begin to really intrigue us. Group dating—where large groups get together—becomes a popular pastime. Kids spend a lot of time talking on the phone and instant messaging each other. The guiding principle here is "safety in numbers." At this age, romantic relationships probably don't develop . . . but meaningful friendships often do begin to form.

- *Stage Three: Are we just friends, or do you like me this week?* At about the age of fourteen or fifteen, many kids really begin to identify strongly with a particular crowd, and the ability to have opposite-sex friendships occurs. These friendships often lead to something more. Group dating gives way to "double dates" and, quite often, to the "first date." We don't need or even want our friends around. Some even experience their first "love" at this age, but that "love" often only lasts a few weeks.

- *Stage Four: Time to meet the parents.* Moving into the later years of high school and the first years of college are when most experience their first "real" or "adult" dating experience. Relationships last longer and we begin to understand what it means to "care" about someone other than ourselves. We invite our significant others to family events; if we are lucky, infatuation is replaced by true emotional connection.

Unfortunately, not every person goes through every stage at the same time, a fact that has been known to cause some adolescent angst and stress. Some kids may skip, miss, or repeat a phase all together. However, going to school and spending time with friends gives everyone the opportunity and the skills to develop some kind of deep, meaningful relationship during the teen years.

A final note: Human beings are a tremendously adaptable, flexible species. The stages I've just outlined are broadly predictable in any cross-section of kids you are likely to find at, say, the shopping mall, but they will vary based on the individual, and, significantly, on family and cultural influences.

While romance can and does occur instantaneously, real relationships take a lot work and are different for everyone. The best advice is simply to stay involved in your teen's life. A word to the wise: most teen sex happens on weekdays after school, not on weekend evenings. This is not so much a matter of you knowing where *they* are as it is a matter of them knowing where *you* are. To the degree that you can, you should make sure a responsible adult is present during these times . . . and whenever your teen needs support and guidance.

20. ENHANCING TEEN CONFIDENCE AND SELF-ESTEEM AFTER A SOCIAL SETBACK

Question: *After trying for, making, and then getting cut from the cheerleading team, my daughter seemed awfully low. She hasn't been herself for weeks. How can I help?*

Teenagers often experience a crisis in confidence when something in their world ignites. The problem event can be as simple as trying a new activity or as complicated as navigating social relationships.

While feelings may be involved, confidence is not primarily about emotions; rather, it is about ability and being good at something. Unfortunately when anyone lacks confidence, it can lead to negative feelings, situational depression, and undue anxiety.

Further complicating this kind of crisis is that it can sometimes be difficult to recognize a teen who lacks confidence. If your angst-ridden adolescent is constantly seeking approval, has few opinions of her own, and/or is always following and never leading, she may be struggling with feelings of low self-worth. Redirecting these negative energies toward a more positive outlook, however, can be easily accomplished.

Highlighting your daughter's strengths will promote positive posturing. Take a look at your teen's inner world to determine where she excels. Engage in conversation about how success in one area can translate to a "nervous area." A student who is good at videogames, for example, is persistent, and this attribute can be applied to many other life activities including school work, extracurriculars, or a job search.

Next, talk with your daughter about looking confident. Self-assured people smile, which also creates internalized relaxed feelings. Strong people make eye contact and appear in control of the situation. Poised people speak with a positive tone and exude strength. It is an old saying, but it has stuck around for decades for a reason: If someone acts confident, then that person will be confident.

Forming positive relationships will also build self-esteem. Joining in new peer activities will allow your daughter to meet like-minded teens and feel good about her personal pursuits, even if participation in another group did not work. Developing relationships with adult mentors such as teachers and coaches will provide strong role models who support your parental concerns. And, of course, spending time with mom and dad is also important. Celebrate your daughter's success, but be sure you also talk about failure by focusing on the positive and future improvement.

Children are not born lacking self-esteem, nor are they born with excessive confidence. These emotions are created around the child's sense of mastery or lack of a sense of mastery. Feelings of poor self-esteem stem from negative attention and non-constructive criticism. Confidence, on the other hand, is built through appropriate praise and growth-promoting activities. Be available for your teen, encourage her to try new things, and explore and celebrate what she is capable of doing well.

21. WHAT IS APPROPRIATE TEEN ATTIRE?

Question: *My teenaged daughter dresses in clothes that make her look too mature, and, I am embarrassed to say, a little too sexy. What do I do?*

Not long ago, I had the opportunity to attend a high school prom. While some girls were dressed in traditional taffeta, many girls wore sleek, stylish and, yes, sexy dresses. Unfortunately, these adolescent girls were sending out mature, grown-up signals that went well beyond their years. Clearly, these intelligent teens had found ways to push the limits of the school's (sensible) dress code with heels that were too high, dresses that were too tight, and makeup that was too sophisticated.

Today's teens live in an extremely fast-paced society, and they receive mixed messages from the media about body image, and about what is and isn't acceptable attire. Yes, one can find appropriately dressed girls on the Disney Channel, but these same young starlets and their ultra-thin model friends are frequently photographed in skintight, skin-baring clothes as they attend Hollywood red carpet events. Given the impact of such messages, the pervasiveness of media in the lives of our teens, and the effect of good old-fashioned peer pressure, today's parent may find it truly difficult to influence her adolescent's choices about attire.

Fortunately, no matter how your daughter dresses, a conversation about current clothing trends is a great way to bond. Talk about the latest fashions and compare them to what was popular in your teenage years. Get out your senior yearbook and show off the styles of your youth, no matter how embarrassing they look now. End the conversation on a positive note, and reflect upon what you yourself have learned about style *before* approaching the more serious subject of clothing that is too sexy.

Clothing is often the way a teen identifies with peers. In fact, most teen girls dress in order to be part of a group, and not to attract the attention of the opposite sex. Unfortunately, appearances project preconceived notions. Many people, especially teen boys, will judge a book by its cover. Ask your teenager to look in the mirror and think about what her style says about her personality.

Talk about how one can look fresh and hip without being overly provocative. If you run into resistance despite your sensible approach, remember that you are the parent. It is okay to "forbid" your daughter from wearing certain clothes; just remember that this conversation can be accomplished in a positive fashion. Let your teen know that it is okay to disagree . . . but that it is also important that you work toward finding an acceptable middle ground. Then engage in some "retail therapy" . . . go shopping!

Have your daughter try on clothes and assist with choosing appropriate styles. If a top shows too much skin, suggest that your trendy teen layer her outfit. If a dress is too short, ask your daughter to try it on with leggings or jeans. Be creative, have lunch, and buy her at least one new outfit. This shows your commitment to promoting a positive image.

In much of our culture, following fashion has replaced good sense. Young girls are relentlessly exposed to trendy style-setting celebrities long before they hit the teenage years, and these celebrities often become role models. It is more difficult for today's parents to educate their impressionable daughters in today's multimedia environment than it was for the parents of past generations. It can be done, however, if you are willing to spend time with your daughter and listen before voicing your concerns and laying down rules.

22. TAKING THE RIGHT RISKS

Question: *How can I help my teen develop a sense of social responsibility?*

A while back, a beloved Shawnee Mission, Kansas, middle school teacher made a mistake. He made an inappropriate comment in the classroom, a bad (in more ways than one) joke that pushed the limits of acceptable classroom banter.

He was fired. What happened next, however, was the real story. Upon hearing that the teacher had been let go, his eighth-grade students came together to protest. Using modern day technology like texting and Facebook, they organized more than fifty kids to picket the school to rehire the teacher. They gathered parents to attend district meetings, and they created a 200-plus person fan page on Facebook to support their cause. These tenacious, tech savvy teens took on the system—and won!

Behaviorally speaking, these students involved themselves in a *positive risk-taking exercise.* Risk-taking usually refers to the tendency to engage in behaviors that may potentially be harmful or dangerous, yet, at the same time, provide the opportunity for some kind of perceived positive outcome. More often we hear about teenagers who engage in what adults would consider negative risky behaviors, such as drug and alcohol use. There are, however, many students, like the ones in this true story, who push the limits by participating in positive risk-taking activities, such as protesting for a cause.

What is so unique about positive risk-taking? It can be a powerful and transformational process that encourages *more* positive behavior. In fact, teens who engage in these types of risks are more likely to avoid alcohol, drugs, and other dangerous activities than teens who do not push themselves to try new and appropriate things.

The moral: Don't just focus on the negative examples of risk-taking that you want your kids to avoid. Encourage your teens to step outside their comfort zone once in a while, too—by, for instance, standing up for some cause they believe in—and help them to see the positive benefits that can result.

23. DEALING WITH TEEN SPORTS ANXIETY

> **Question:** *My son is extremely worried about how he will perform in an upcoming high school baseball playoff game. How can I help?*

A high school baseball coach recently asked me to help reduce the anxiety of his players, particularly as they step into the batter box. As I reviewed my strategies with the team, it became apparent these ideas were much bigger than the game itself and could be applied metaphorically to everyday life. Feel free to share these tips with your son . . . and you may find that he uses them not only for the big game, but for other potentially stressful events, as well.

- *Take care of your body.* Sleep is essential especially before a big game, because it allows your mind and your body to be at their best. In addition, you should eat a healthful breakfast and lunch on the big day, and consume healthful snacks with a lot of protein. Avoid caffeine. Stay hydrated! Drink plenty of water.

- *Practice.* Develop automaticity! This is the ability to perform complex tasks without thinking about them on a conscious level. Practice your swing over and over and over again. When you do get to the plate, don't think about your swing. That takes your focus away from the task at hand. Just hit the ball.

- *Positive self-talk and success visualization.* Positive self-talk can be used to correct bad habits, focus attention, build self-confidence, and change negative thoughts to positive ones. Mental imagery is the process of using one's senses to create or recreate a positive or successful past experience in the mind. Tell yourself you can hit the ball and visualize yourself doing it well. This process will build confidence.

- *Focus/Attention.* When you are at bat, only the pitcher and the ball matter. Not the score, not the standings, not your last time up to the plate. Be in the moment. The ability to selectively attend to important cues, events, or thoughts, and tune out others, is one of the keys to successful performance.

- *Set Goals.* Successful people in all professions and sports set goals, both short-term and long-term. They write them down, review them regularly, and make sure the goals are realistic and measurable. If you don't have goals, how will you know you are getting better?

- *Relax.* You can recognize anxiety and learn how to control it through relaxation strategies. Among the best and simplest relaxation strategies are deep-breathing exercises. Deep breathing is an instantaneous process that can be used throughout the day, and right before batting. Before each game, you may also want to consider meditation (relaxing the mind first and letting the muscles follow), and progressive relaxation techniques (relaxing the muscles first, and letting the mind follow).

- *Remember: You can't be perfect.* Not all batters hit all balls. It is okay to be frustrated by bad at-bats, but don't hyper-focus on them or use them as excuses to put yourself down. Learn from your mistakes.

You can manage stress effectively by breaking the game process down into three phases: *Preparation* (pregame mindset and nutrition), *execution* (being your best during the game), and *evaluation* (postgame analysis used to improve for the next time).

24. TRAVELING WITH TEENS

> **Question:** *Our kids are teenagers now, and planning family outings isn't as much fun as it used to be. It seems that their idea of a vacation now differs from ours. What can we do to ensure that the whole family has a great time this summer?*

It's not your imagination. When your teenagers were tots, traveling *was* much simpler. A sandy beach with the occasional kid-friendly activity was all the family needed to have a good time. Now, however, your young children have become young adults, and the family vacation has become a complex subject of negotiation, as two generations squabble over what to do. To pave the way for a relaxing and rejuvenating vacation, do some advance planning and allow your teen a say in the decision about where to stay.

Specifically, you should include your teenagers at the very start of the planning process. Discuss what they want from a vacation *before* choosing a destination. Generate a variety of options, taking their objectives and preferences into account, and present the choices to the kids. Over a family dinner, discuss each locale and let your excited adolescents guide the way to family fun.

Once the location has been decided, let the aspiring vacationers plan a whole day's worth of activities. Encourage your teens to research activity options; let them create a complete schedule of events, including transportation and dining options. For this to work, parents must commit to the plan even if it means doing something outrageously adventurous, or—here's the hard part—"wasting" the morning with a late sleep. (Remember, their brains need more sleep than a grownup's.) Typically, teens will make good choices when given this responsibility; allowing them to own a piece of the planning ensures minimal complaining and maximum enjoyment.

Turnabout is fair play, of course. Parents should also participate in the plan-a-day process, but should add a twist. Choose an afternoon for you and/or your spouse to spend one-on-one quality alone time with each of your children. This can be as simple as a hike up a mountain or as exciting as a surfing lesson. The goal is to choose something that you can enjoy together. Mixing it up in this way promotes family bonding and creates great dinner conversation as each "team" shares stories from the day.

All of the advance planning in the world, however, will not guarantee a peaceful getaway unless a family conversation regarding trip rules and expectations takes place. This, too, should happen before the departure date. Remind your traveling teens that all the home rules still apply: no smoking, no drinking, no cursing, and no hitting your siblings. Emphasize the importance of time: what time teens need to return in the evening, what time tired teens actually need to wake up in the morning (be generous), and what kind of time teens must spend with mom and dad. Set some basic ground rules and discuss your teens' concerns as they arise.

Taking all of these steps will help you to ensure that travel time is a blast and make it more likely that everyone will get along all right. Vacations are worth planning for, both because they provide a needed break from the "everyday" and because they can provide some of life's most memorable moments. Savor the time, leave life's worries behind, and take lots of pictures. Bon Voyage!

25. CAN A TEEN LAND A SUMMER JOB IN TODAY'S TOUGH MARKET?

Question: *My son says I'm pressuring him too hard to find summer work. I say it's time to step up and take some responsibility. Who's right?*

It's quite possible that you're both right . . .but I would urge you to be as supportive as you possibly can in discussions about summer employment, and to avoid issuing ultimatums and orders to your son.

As this book goes to press, the job market for teens is slow. Many jobs traditionally given to teens are going to older workers who are willing to take low-paying employment to make ends meet. What's more, establishments that usually recruit teens as summer help (retail, theme parks, and the hospitality industry) are the very places where Americans hit by the recession are cutting back on their spending.

Even without a down economy, finding work as a teen can be hard. Parents demanding that a teenager "show some initiative" by going out and finding a job need to realize what a difficult task it may be to find work. Finding a job, after all, is a job in itself.

How does a teen land a summer job in today's tough market? Here are a few suggestions you can share with your son.

- *Get mom or dad to help you put together a simple resume.* You do have something to brag about, you just need to figure out what it is. A solid resume sets you apart from other job seekers because it shows you have thought ahead, taken initiative, and done something different.

- *Look presentable, because first impressions do matter.* You don't always need to wear a suit, but you do need to dress like you deserve a job!

- *Act like an adult by speaking and acting properly.* No profanity or crude humor. Say "Yes, sir" or "Yes, ma'am." Look prospective employers in the eye, and shake hands firmly.

- *Be prepared to keep going after you hear a "no."* Finding a job is a right place/right time deal in the best of times. Don't take rejection personally. It is part of the process.

- *Follow up.* Ask for the manager's card. Send a snail-mail note or at least a short email after your meeting. Check back in person the next week.

- *Put a new twist on an old tradition.* Use social media to build your employment network. Get on Facebook and ask your friends if they know who might be hiring.

- *Work for free–seriously.* Volunteering for a cause is rewarding, but you should also consider trying on your dream job for size. For example, if you want to be a lawyer, knock on some doors and offer to assist at no charge. Treat this opportunity like a job, and who knows? You may eventually get paid. Whether you do or not, this will build great resume material.

- *Start a business.* It's easier than you think. Work the neighborhood and offer to do odd jobs. This is a great way to meet others in your community and learn how to build a business from the ground up. If you get the right help—say, from mom or dad—you might just learn some important lessons about marketing, bookkeeping, and customer service.

- *Check out summer job websites.* For the industrious older teen, there are some really interesting opportunities out there. Some of the most intriguing may even involve travel and high adventure. You can talk over all the opportunities with mom and dad. For the younger teen, you can start thinking about jobs now . . . and lay the groundwork for a strong application next summer.

http://www.snagajob.com

http://www.aplus-summerjobs.com/

http://www.coolworks.com/

http://getthatgig.com/

THE WORLD BEYOND:

Questions About School

---

26. TEENS AND STUDYING

> **Question:** *My son's grades weren't so good last year. With the school year starting, how can I help my son to be a better student and study more efficiently?*

I recently asked a group of high school freshmen how they study. The answers were both diverse and fascinating. One student commented that he studies only the big points because "the little stuff doesn't matter." Another told me he just stares at his book for fifteen minutes or so before taking a break. Still another told me she looks for the "bold" words in the textbook to learn and memorize.

These ideas are creative solutions, but they are also ineffective methods for cultivating a student's skills. Traditional values related to scheduling and environment are one important tool for dealing with the demands of a high school career. At the same time, students should develop their own study style while adhering to "old school" principles.

Time management is the first step. Consider that most teens spend at least thirty-five hours a week in classes, have extracurricular activities, and engage in life activities such as doctor appointments, social activities, and household chores. They've also been known to spend time playing video and computer games. Balancing homework hours with other activities is a crucial concept to school success. This means taking time to plan intelligently. If your son doesn't have at least an informal plan for spending the available hours in the day, then he won't have the time he needs. Teens should track both daily assignments and long-term projects, using a planner to schedule due dates and outside activities.

When a student studies turns out to be quite important to knowledge retention. Some people need to complete homework before relaxing, while others prefer an after-school break. Once they are comfortably engaged in academic pursuits, teens should prioritize the importance of work, starting with the most difficult tasks and working their way toward the most familiar material.

Learning occurs best when the body and brain are rested and alert. This means getting a good night's sleep before studying is absolutely essential!

The proper ambiance will also help keep your teen on task. Soft, comfortable couches may create an environment that is too relaxed and not conducive to focused work. For most students, studying should take place at a large desk in a well-lit room. The study area should be stocked with pens, pencils, paper and other essential aids. Provide nearby access to healthful snacks and water. This will help your teen avoid succumbing to the desire to take a trip to another part of the house . . . and getting distracted.

Don't hesitate to monitor your kid's progress . . . tactfully. The occasional walk-by in a passive, non-confrontational manner will go a long way toward ensuring that your teen stays on task. Knowing mom is just around the corner will help to dissuade him or her from any impulse to stare into space . . . or engage in some clandestine technological diversion.

Have a conversation with your teen about what works best and what the potential problem areas are.

Learning to study is an evolutionary process that needs adjustment along the way. Celebrate the successes and look for the chance to learn together from the occasional mistakes.

27. SUPPORTING YOUR TEEN'S EDUCATIONAL SUCCESS

> **Question:** *My eighth-grader is getting ready to go back to school. How can I help make sure the academic year is a successful one for her?*

Different kids have different needs. Below are some general guidelines as well as some specific suggestions to make sure the return to class is a positive experience.

- *Get sleeping and eating schedules back on track.* Two to three weeks before school starts, begin "training" and "preparing" for the school schedule. Your goal is to get your teen to go to sleep and wake up in the morning as though it were a school day. This will help minimize problems with first week crankiness. Begin preparing healthier foods; make more time for family meals. Encourage your kids to have lunch at the same time they would during the school day.

- *Plan after-school time.* Discuss homework rules and schedules *before* the school year begins; this will help you to avoid later arguments. Figure out what time your kids should start working, and predetermine the consequences for when these goals are not met. Collaborate with the kids about what they will do about sign-ups, tryout schedules, and time management issues connected to extracurricular activities.

- *Get an early start on back-to-school shopping.* It's time to purge the closets and determine what new clothes and outfits your child needs for the new year. Find out what needs to be replaced, as well as what needs to be purchased for the first time. Organize a day with the kids to have lunch and go shopping.

- *Check out the calendar.* Review the school calendar and identify the most critical dates and times. What are the hours of the first few days of school? When are back-to-school nights and parent conferences? What are the dates of important tests like the ACT and SAT? While you're at it, schedule school physicals, eye exams, and hearing tests if you have not already done so. Waiting until the last minute can cause stress.

- *Hit the books early.* Make sure any summer reading or similar schoolwork is completed a couple of weeks before school starts.

The back-to-school period is not just about the kids; it affects the entire family. Prepare well, stay organized, and set clear boundaries, and you will help to ensure a stress-free start to the new school year for everybody.

28. DEALING WITH BACK-TO-SCHOOL ANXIETY

> **Question:** *My daughter seems extremely anxious about going back to school. What can we do to help her?*

Whenever there is change, anxiety is a natural response. Back-to-school is particularly likely to cause mixed emotions, as kids are both excited and anxious about returning to school. Seeing friends, sharing summer stories, and going on back-to-school shopping trips can make the start of the school year fun. On the other hand, uncertainty and self-doubt causes some students to be very nervous indeed as the fall semester begins.

As the school year looms, kids are likely to worry about social groups, emotional issues, academics, and safety concerns, to name just a few. Back-to-school anxieties typically fall into two broad categories: the "whos" and the "enoughs." The "whos" are questions like:

- Who will my teachers be?

- Who will be in my class?

- Who will sit next to me at lunch?

The "enoughs" may include questions like:

- Am I good enough to make the team?

- Am I smart enough to get good grades?

- Am I cool enough not to be bullied?

Below are a few tips that can help you help your son or daughter to ease back into the school routine and reduce those first-day jitters.

- *Validate your child's anxiety and listen to wor-*

ries without dismissing them. If your teen needs to cry, let him; that may be the ticket to feeling better.

- *Involve your anxious adolescent in the back-to-school campaign.* Take your teen school shopping, discuss schedules, and highlight the good things about the first weeks of school. Accentuate the positive! Reinforce the good things like seeing old friends, taking part in a favorite sport or activity, and starting fresh. Don't remind kids of last year's pitfalls.

- *If you feel the anxiety problem is major*, discuss your concerns with the school counselors and/or teachers. School anxiety is a normal experience for some kids during the teen years, but remember that it should be a temporary issue. If the problem persists, consider getting professional assistance from a therapist.

29. PRIVATE VS. PUBLIC SCHOOL — WHICH IS RIGHT FOR YOUR TEEN?

Question: *Should we spend the money to send my daughter to a private school?*

Many families agonize over the difficult decision of where their teens should attend school. Some choose public education, a choice that may be based on economics or on political convictions. Others opt for private institutions based on the desire to get into a good college, or on a family legacy. No matter your opinion, you should consider all the options as you create a plan.

First, consider practicality. What are all the costs? Public school is free, and private school tuition can range from a few thousand dollars to upward of twenty grand per year. Make sure you can afford the *entire* high school experience, meaning all four years. Changing midway could be a big challenge for your daughter.

How far will your child have to travel to attend the desired school? A long commute can affect attendance, limit extracurricular activities, and shrink the social network of nearby friends.

Does your child have a physical, emotional, or learning concern that is a better fit for a particular school? Both public and private schools can excel at meeting special needs, but some schools service specific requirements better than others.

Next, consider what is personally important to you and your teen. Does the school offer the desired curriculum? Most schools offer at least a few advanced placement courses and technical classes. Make sure the facility will nurture and challenge your child's special interest area, whatever it is: science, art, or auto mechanics.

How important are athletics and extracurricular participation? Some private schools with the "best" programs only provide opportunities for the most gifted in any given extracurricular field, while others have "no cut" policies offering everyone an opportunity to participate.

What learning atmosphere will suit your teen best? Think about the benefits of a low student-teacher ratio, a religious curriculum (if that's what you're after), block scheduling, academic rigor, and student diversity, to name just a few factors.

Once you have generated the criteria for a successful student-school match, visit school(s) you are considering. Most will offer open house days for prospective pupils and their parents. Many private schools hold "high school nights," where representatives from a multitude of educational establishments give short presentations. If your public school hosts one of these events, bring your teen and discuss the prospective placements at the end of the evening.

Most important, once you and your daughter narrow the field, have her spend some time shadowing a student at her top three choices. This academic "test drive" will provide insights into campus life that will be invaluable when you sit down to make this important decision together.

Choosing a public or private education is an important choice for your daughter and you. The only bad decision will be one that is made impulsively and without full discussion of the issues. Staying appropriately involved and communicating with your teen about her education is the best way to ensure academic and emotional success, no matter what school she attends.

30. IS YOUR KID BEING BULLIED?

> **Question:** *The period between the time he leaves the house and the time he gets to school is the most traumatic time of the day for my son. I can tell by his body language as he gets ready each morning that he's getting ready for trouble. He doesn't like to talk about it, but from what his younger sister tells me, I think he is being bullied on the bus. What can I do?*

Not long ago, a student in a suburb of St. Louis was beaten on a school bus because of his seat choice. A brave high school senior intervened to help stop the fight.

Unfortunately, bus time is one of the most common settings for bullying. If your son is a victim of a school bus bully, there are a few simple strategies that may help. For instance, you might suggest to your son that he sit in the front of the bus, that he makes sure he sits around friends, and that he tells the bully to stop in a clear, concise way that is loud enough for everyone on the bus to hear.

Of course, you should document all concerns and contact the school authorities to inform them of the problem as you understand it to be affecting your son.

There are lots of great resources available online for parents who believe their kids may be being bullied. One of my favorites is the federal government's StopBullying.org site, which offers the following sound advice on "bully-proofing your child":

- Bullying is not a normal rite of passage. It can have serious consequences.

- You can help your child learn how to prevent bullying. These tips can help:

- Help your child understand bullying. Explain what bullying is. It is more than physical; it can be done in person or over the phone or computer.

- Keep open lines of communication with your child. Check in with your child and listen to any concerns about friends and other students.

- Encourage your child to pursue their interests. Doing what they love may help your child be more confident among their peers and make friends with other kids with similar interests.

- Teach your child to take a stand against bullying. Give guidance about how to stand up to those who bully if it is safe to do so.

- Talk to your child about seeking help from a trusted adult when feeling threatened by a bully. Talk about whom they should go to for help and role-play what they should say. Assure your child that they should not be afraid to tell an adult when someone they know is being bullied.

- Know what is going on in your child's school. Visit the school website, subscribe to the student paper—if there is one—and join the PTA listserve or mailing list. Get to know other parents, school counselors, and staff. Contact the school by phone or e-mail if you have suggestions to make the school a safer and better learning place.

31. MEAN GIRLS

> **Question:** *Some of my daughter's friends seem to be teasing her more than they should. She appears to me to be hurt by this, but always tells me there is nothing wrong. Could she be hiding her feelings?*

Girls can be just as aggressive as boys. In fact, some might consider female hostility in school more dramatic and damaging than boy bullying. Girls antagonize in a covert, complex, and long-term manner; boys, on the other hand, are overt, obnoxious, and immediate. In addition, girls are likely to employ cruel, socially manipulative tactics that involve group dynamics—tactics that can cause good friends to become instant enemies.

Relational aggression is a growing area of concern for today's teen, and the typical type of hurtful behavior most frequently used in female circles. This is bullying with a social twist. It means using exclusionary tactics to inflict hurt on others, by (for instance) crowding an unwanted victim out of a lunch table spot, encouraging friends to give a cold shoulder, and spreading inappropriate rumors. The results are internal scars that may take years to heal. Unfortunately, most girls fall victim to one or more forms of this behavior at some point during the high school years.

The first and most important thing to do is to keep lines of communication with your daughter open, and improve communication over time. Pay close attention to how your daughter acts; keep an eye out for changes in behavior that will help you to determine whether she is a target of a really mean girl. Look for dropping grades; listen to the language she uses to describe her day. Do your teen's comments indicate that she wants to switch schools and escape her world? Is she acting overly tough to mask the source of some undisclosed pain? Is she fearful that her relational problems will never end? These are signs of a distressed daughter who is facing intense inner turmoil.

Because girls tend to be overly critical of themselves, they really need the support of their families and friends to develop defenses against daily social dramas. Empathize with your daughter's distress, assure her that you are there for her, and discuss relationship-building strategies that will help her to win allies at school. For instance, you might suggest that your daughter offer authentic compliments for the accomplishments of her peers. This is a sign of confidence that others will respond to with a positive attitude. In addition, you should:

- Discuss how joining with others can help your teen reach her goals and build positive relationships based on success. Group studying sessions, for example, are more rewarding, and likelier to build friends, than lonely late-night learning.

• Emphasize the importance of open and honest communication. Your daughter may need practice speaking up when she doesn't like someone else's threatening or inappropriate behavior. Not all confrontation is bad; in fact, some is essential for healthy development. Confronting a situation while maintaining a sense of self-respect and respect for others, and working toward problem resolution, are major life skills. Practicing them with her peers—and with you—will help your daughter learn to de-escalate issues in a mature manner.

• You should also encourage your daughter to engage in a wider variety of activities. Students who have multiple friends tend to cope better with drama, because they have more social supports.

Determining whether your daughter is a victim of relational aggression may be quite difficult, but stick with it. Again, staying connected with regular family time and frequent conversation is the best way to encourage open communication about this or any problem.

32. WHAT TEST TO TAKE?

Question: *My daughter does not know whether she should take the ACT, SAT or both. How does she decide?*

You finally learned what LOL, OMG and BTW means. Now, your daughter is in high school, and there is another set of acronyms to learn: PSAT, PLAN, ACT, and SAT. You may be among the parents who think they do not need Google to determine the initial meaning of these things, but a little further examination is required if you are to truly understand the impact these tests will have on your child.

The ACT (American College Testing Program) and the SAT (Scholastic Aptitude Reasoning Test) are designed to evaluate students and predict college success, but each accomplishes this differently. Which test to take can be a stressful question for an emerging high school graduate.

Philosophically, the ACT and SAT approach academic assessment from completely different directions. The ACT tests what one has been taught in school, taking a curriculum-based approach. The SAT, on the other hand, is more focused on assessing innate aptitudes; it tests general reasoning skills and problem-solving abilities. The goal of both tests, however, is the same: to determine college readiness.

In addition to the philosophical differences, the assessment structures of these two tests are also quite different. The ACT is pure multiple choice. There are no penalties for guessing or marking wrong answers. The SAT has not only multiple choice questions, but also an essay and "grid-in" math question where a student actually writes in the correct response. There is also a quarter-point penalty for every wrong answer. Answers left blank are not scored.

Still unsure which test your student should take? Consider the curricular aspects when making an informed choice. The ACT has four specific categories covering math, science, English, and reading, with an optional essay. The SAT focuses on math abilities, critical reading skills, required essay writing, and a variety of optional subject area tests. Content-wise, the ACT has trigonometry and a full science section; the SAT has neither. In the area of language, the ACT focuses on grammar and punctuation, whereas the SAT is steeped in vocabulary.

If your daughter is a good test-taker, it doesn't really matter which exam she chooses. Many students who test well take both exams. On the other hand, students who struggle, have anxiety, or simply don't want to sit for both have another option that can help them to decide. These teens should review their performance on the PLAN (pre-ACT) and

PSAT (pre-SAT) tests. Both are precursors to their perspective assessments and both are good predictors of future performance. If a student opts to take only one test, she should choose the one better suited to her strengths.

Make sure that your daughter knows the testing requirements of the colleges that she may want to attend before making her final decision. Choose wisely, because college acceptance and scholarship dollars will be influenced by test scores.

Q & A:
SPECIAL
CHALLENGES

Every teen experiences challenges . . . but some challenges can be more intimidating, and potentially dangerous, than others. In this part of the Playbook, you will find clear answers to some of the toughest questions parents can face, and practical guidance that will help you make the very best choices for your teen and your whole family.

SPECIAL CHALLENGES:
Questions About Learning Problems

---

33. MAKING SENSE OF LEARNING DISABILITIES

Question: *My daughter's teacher just informed me that she wants to have my daughter evaluated for a possible learning disability. I'm a little uneasy about this. What exactly does it mean? What can I expect?*

This kind of question comes up a lot from parents who have not yet been through the evaluation process with their child. There is really nothing to be uneasy about. This request from your daughter's teacher is evidence that the "system is working" and that the school is doing its best to make it easy for your daughter to do well in class. Below is a general description of what you are likely to encounter during the evaluation process.

Diagnostic Interview. This interview will ask about your daughter's experience in school, and about any record of prior accommodations or auxiliary aides, including any information about specific conditions under which the accommodations were used. It will also feature an extensive review of historical grades, academic issues, and standardized test scores.

Aptitude Test. This is a complete intellectual assessment, with all subtests and standard core scores reported. These assessments would include either of the most recent and age-appropriate versions of the Wechsler Intelligence Test (which I prefer) and/or the Woodcock-Johnson Psychoeducational Battery-Revised: Tests of Cognitive Ability.

Academic Achievement Assessment. This is a comprehensive academic achievement assessment with various subtests. The battery includes current levels of academic functioning in relevant areas such as reading (decoding and comprehension), mathematics, oral language, and written language. These assessments are either the most recent and age appropriate version of the Woodcock-Johnson Psychoeducational Battery-Revised: Tests of Achievement (preferred) or the Wechsler Individual Achievement Test. Additional formal tests such as the most recent and age-appropriate version of the Grey Oral Reading Test, the Test of Written Language, or other academic assessments are often integrated with the above assessment. It all sounds complicated, but the goal here is actually pretty straightforward: to assist in determining the presence of a learning disability, and, if there is a disability, to differentiate it from coexisting disorders.

Information Processing. This part of the assessment tests specific areas of information processing (for example, short- and long-term memory, sequential memory, auditory and visual perception/processing, processing speed, executive function, and motor ability). There are a variety of potential assessments that may be used here, such as the Woodcock-Johnson Psychoeducational Battery-Revised: Tests of Cognitive Ability and the Connors Continuous Processing Test.

Behavioral Assessment. This is a measurement of mental health issues which uses questionnaires and behavioral scales to rule out other conditions that may co-exist with learning concerns. (This is not used to diagnosis psychological issues.)

Specific Diagnosis. If there is a learning disability, you and your daughter will find out what it is in this part of the assessment. If there isn't, you'll learn that here, too.

Clinical Summary. This is a diagnostic summary based on the comprehensive evaluation. It's included in the report to determine the presence of a specific learning disability or ADHD, specifically as it relates to your daughter's educational setting.

All of the above is undertaken to help school officials get your daughter exactly what she needs in order to get the most out of her school experience. Assure your daughter—and yourself—that the evaluation process is there not to judge anyone, but to make learning easier.

34. WHEN KIDS WANT TO QUIT

> **Question:** My son wants to quit playing soccer. He has played for almost ten years. It seems odd to me that he would simply walk away from something he has put so much time, effort, and energy into perfecting. Is this decision of his a signal that something is wrong, or is this kind of change typical for his age?

It's typical of many teens—but a lot depends on how your son disengaged from the sport.

Parents sometimes forget that being a teenager is a full-time job. Most of them spend more than thirty hours a week at school and engage in a variety of other pursuits, including part-time jobs, music lessons, and sports. Other teens, however, choose to drop after-school adventures in favor of "chillaxin'", spending time with technology, and, yes, avoiding their parents. As school becomes more time-consuming and friends become more important, former pursuits of pleasure often turn into distant memories.

It can be difficult for parents to convince their children to stay committed to an old activity or become excited about something new, but research shows that some kind of outside interest is good for kids and worth your tactful advocacy. Teenagers who participate in some kind of extracurricular activity are less likely to abuse drugs or alcohol or become teen parents. (It's worth reminding ourselves here that one of the reasons many parents make sure that the hours between 2:30 and 6:00 are filled with some kind of structured activity is that this is the peak period for teen sexual activity.)

Kids who have outside activities have more developed social skills, stronger problem-solving abilities, and make better grades than those who don't. That much is not in dispute. The larger question I hear from parents is: Should I be the "pushy" parent who forces my teen to engage, or should I be the "push-over" parent who accepts passively my teen's nonparticipation in any kind of extracurricular activity?

The best answer is "Neither." It is difficult to force a teenager to do anything; however, a well-timed and carefully choreographed conversation can offer you some insight into your teen's current thinking . . . and encourage him to make good decisions.

The first step is to ask your teen why he wants to stop an activity that was previously a passion. The second step is to listen and wait for his words. Too many parents try to fill an awkward silence with adult wisdom. Allow your teen the time and space he needs to explain what is going on in his mind.

Some adolescents end their involvements with long-term activities because they are uncomfortable in their present situation. These teens may fear failure because they are not as good as the other kids, or they may stop because they lack the dedication to stay competitive, or they may choose to drop out because the new coach is too harsh. In these situations, it is best to listen and assist where you can with problem-solving strategies. Your son may actually want to continue but be unsure about how to proceed.

Other teens quit because they simply want to try something new. After years of playing a particular sport, they decide that acting in a play or joining the school newspaper is just what they need. In this case, your job is pretty clear-cut. Support your teen's new passion, even if it is different from your own interests.

Then there are the teens who stop participating but can't tell you why. Quitting may be an indicator that your son is struggling emotionally. Look for signs of stress such as illness, fatigue, or dropping grades. Are there any other behaviors or emotions from your teen that concern you? (Note the discussion of frequency, duration, and intensity that appears in question 39.) If you sense a deeper problem, contact the school and talk to his teachers. If these professionals notice behavioral changes, it may be time to seek outside additional assistance.

It is developmentally important for adolescents to regularly participate in self-esteem-building adventures and fun after-school activities. At some point, however, your child may want to quit. Make sure to ask why . . . and listen to the answer you receive. If you do, you will help your teen maintain a healthy balance between school, activities, and family.

35. TEEN ADHD

Question: *My son is in the tenth grade. During the past year he seems to have become much more impulsive and easily distractible. Can students this old have ADHD?*

This is a difficult question. Adolescents with Attention Deficit/Hyperactivity Disorder (ADHD) may act impulsively, be easily distracted, and have difficulty focusing . . . but this is not necessarily specific to ADHD. Anxious kids may also be hyper and restless, depressed kids may also be inattentive and disorganized, and typical teens may display all of the above behaviors! So how are parents to know whether their teen is experiencing turbulent times . . . or behaving in developmentally appropriate ways?

ADHD behaviors can go unnoticed during the elementary school years, because these students are often extremely intelligent and can develop independent compensating strategies for their attention deficits. Note, too, that experienced grade-school teachers are particularly talented at helping young children stay on task. Maturing students, however, face new challenges as they encounter teachers who require more focused attention in class, juggle the demands of a busier scholastic schedule, attempt more demanding academic tasks, and negotiate increased independence. Grades may drop, and attention problems may become more noticeable, during the high school years.

An accurate assessment begins by meeting with a qualified professional. While a pediatrician's perspective may initially be helpful, their diagnostic process typically lacks the depth of someone who specializes in ADHD diagnosis. Your son needs a comprehensive evaluation, a multi-layered process that not only confirms the presence of ADHD, but also provides insight into how his attention issues affect his thinking and learning.

The first step toward a proper diagnosis is having an up-to-date medical physical, hearing test, and vision screening to ensure that other potential problems have been ruled out. Next, meet with a qualified diagnostician who will review academic records, interview the family, and consult with the school. This professional will also provide behavioral questionnaires for the teachers, parents, and student, as well as administer a comprehensive set of intelligence, academic, and ADHD-specific assessments. Parents should expect to receive a detailed diagnostic report soon after the process is completed.

The good news is that ADHD students can be just as successful as their peers. Detailed testing will provide data that can assist families with providing the appropriate support and securing the necessary school accommodations. Yes, the testing is time-consuming and can be expensive, but before one considers more aggressive options, such as medication, it is best to have all the facts.

A final note: Multiple studies indicate that ADHD is typically genetic. The next time your teen makes an impulsive, poor decision or does not pay attention to your comments, there is a very good chance mom or dad is at least partly "responsible" for the situation, too. It's in the genes! Knowing this can help you provide support, guidance, and empathy for your teen.

SPECIAL CHALLENGES:

Questions About Compulsive Behaviors

---

36. IS FACEBOOK HARMFUL TO YOUR TEEN'S HEALTH?

Question: *I heard something on the news about potential emotional problems linked to the use of social media forums. My daughter spends a lot of time on Facebook. What should I be watching out for?*

According to a published report in the *Journal of Pediatrics* entitled "Clinical Report: The Impact of

Social Media on Children, Adolescents, and Families" there is a growing concern about a new phenomenon known as "Facebook depression."

This is defined by mental health professionals as "depression that develops when preteens and teens spend a great deal of time on social media sites, such as Facebook, and then begin to exhibit classic signs of depression."

While many of us use the internet to enhance life through activities like online shopping, bill-paying, and catching up on our interest areas, there is a "dark" side to the online world that parents should know about, too. It is common knowledge that many people suffer from internet addictions affiliated with gambling, pornography, and videogames. Now, however, there is also research indicating that heavy social media use could be a problem.

The issue is a controversial one. There is an ongoing debate among mental health professionals about whether using Facebook and other social media outlets could actually be the cause of depression . . . or whether that depressive state existed in the teens in question prior to their going online. While this is an interesting topic, which side of the debate you believe is not as important as developing an understanding of the unique challenges that portals like Facebook could create for an adolescent.

The online universe can be an intense, emotionally-charged world for teens, and many of them may measure their own personal self-worth through the lens of some extremely unrealistic cyber-perceptions. Numerical friend tallies, pictures of partying peers, and online postings can injure self-esteem if a sensitive teen is not included in the fun. Many teens who view these pages conclude that their life is comparatively inadequate. Additionally, a lot of kids think of Facebook as a popularity contest: Who can have the most connections and post the coolest pics? Unfortunately, as in many socially-driven contests among middle schoolers and high school students, this process generates not only victories but also defeats.

Consider, for instance, that Facebook is a place where teens can announce their accomplishments and receive accolades from their friends and family for their most recent accomplishments. This is an excellent way to use Facebook, and I would certainly encourage loved ones to participate in this manner. On the opposite end of the spectrum, however, imagine the student who feels he has nothing to post and/or nobody to comment about his successes. Further enhancing this teen's downward spiral of depression could be projected feelings that others think he is a "loser" because of his inability to participate in the various celebrations.

There are no easy answers here. There are only parents who engage and support their kids online and parents who don't. If your daughter is spending time on Facebook, it is definitely worth your while to spend some time there as well—and to talk face-to-face with her about what kind of messages she wants to get. Many teens prefer to receive email messages from parents and other family members, rather than public postings.

Why bother following your teen's behavior online and talking to her about her experiences? One excellent reason is that cyber-bullies can and do sink their victims to a new low. While face-to-face bully behaviors can have long lasting emotional affects, the physical assault ends upon the conclusion of the incident. Online harassment, however, is typically public, humiliating, and, potentially at least, capable of remaining in cyberspace forever. This can make it difficult for students to recover or escape from an incident.

Using social media is one of the most common activities that kids engage in today. Research has also indicated that online interactions can have many benefits, including better technical skills, enhanced communication abilities, and stronger social connections. If, however, your teen is not part of the "in crowd," social media may end up emphasizing her "outsider" status, and that could lead to depression, anxiety, and other mental health concerns. (See also Question 40.)

37. TEENS AND OBESITY

> **Question:** *My son is seriously overweight, and he's very sensitive about it. I have been cautious, maybe too cautious, about hurting his self-esteem, and thus haven't said much. How should I approach this issue?*

Parents have difficulty approaching their teenagers about any number of difficult subjects, but weight issues appear to be among the trickiest.

Let's start with one of the biggest problems—thankfully, one you seem to have avoided. I'm talking about pet names and "terms of endearment" that focus (thoughtlessly) on body image. These are often internalized as criticisms. An affectionate parent may call their overweight child "chunky monkey," "marshmallow man," or "butterball," but a distraught child will often perceive this name as a subtle, or not-so-subtle, insult.

Well-intentioned hints such as "diet more," "just eat less," "take only half," and "avoid sweets" may appear to be helpful, yet overweight teens resent these types of suggestions. This advice is common knowledge, too general to be of any practical use, and tend to drive teens away from the trusted adults in their life. Not knowing whom to talk to, many will simply retreat to the privacy and stress-free environment of their bedroom . . . to indulge in hidden snacks.

If your teen is significantly overweight, the first thing to do is seek professional help. Discuss the situation with the doctor or pediatrician; find out if a medical concern could be the cause of the excessive weight gain. After physical problems have been ruled out, you may choose to seek the assistance of a therapeutic professional. Kids often eat in response to some type of stressor. If the issue can be identified, your teen can learn better coping strategies.

Consider that you yourself may not be modeling good eating habits. At dinner time, parents should cook healthful, well-balanced meals. Instead of allowing family members to serve themselves, try making up plates with sensible portions. Set a good example by limiting your own food intake. The alternative: perpetuating the unhealthy cycle that may have caused the problem in the first place. If mom and dad load up on extra calories, children will follow.

Plan fun, active family outings that everyone can enjoy. Rememeber that overweight kids often have negative attitudes toward exercise because their weight sometimes makes it difficult to participate, or because they have learned to expect verbal abuse during PE class. Keep the activity accessible for everyone; keep the atmosphere light. Engage kids in lively activities that encourage movement and promote coordination. You might take a family bike ride in the park, throw a ball in the backyard, or learn to roller-skate or ice-skate.

The most effective way to help overweight children and teens is through good communication, family intervention, and positive support. Trying to scare your kids into losing weight is definitely not a good idea: this does far more harm than good, often causing angst-ridden adolescents to become depressed or anxious, or adults with eating-disorders. Bear in mind that someone else, usually a peer, is in all likelihood already giving your son a hard time about his weight. Don't join the chorus.

You may not have as much control as you'd like about what happens at school around body image and self-esteem issues, but you can create a positive, supportive environment at home.

38. TEEN GAMBLING

> **Question**: *My son seems to be spending a lot of time playing poker with his friends. He also reads about it on the Internet and watches it on TV. Could he have a gambling problem?*

Most kids are exposed to gambling long before they reach the adolescent years. They bet their friends that they can run faster, make a basket, or choose the winning team. They play chance games at fast-food restaurants with lucky scratch-off cards, or look under the caps of carbonated beverages to win a prize. You may have made an innocent wager with your child without even realizing it.

Today's generation is the first to grow up with large-scale legalized gaming. In one form or another, gambling has now been legalized in every state of the Union. Whether gambling takes the form of a casino, a lottery, or a casual sports bet, games of chance have become a major part of popular culture.

Further extending the reach of this highly profitable industry is the Internet, which offers anyone the opportunity to "make a bet" with virtually no regulations regarding age, competency, or ability to avoid a problem with compulsive behavior.

Most kids like to make the occasional bet, and find wagering to be a fun but forgettable experience. What distinguishes social gambling from problem betting has more to do with the individual than it does with a single activity, like rolling the dice. Unfortunately, approximately eleven percent of teens admit to gambling regularly, and one in fifty teens has a true addiction.

The best way to prevent gaming addiction is to be engaged in your teen's life, to pay attention, and to converse with your kids tactfully about fiscal awareness. Explain how the family budget works. Let your teens know that there are things you want but can't afford. Emphasize the importance of relationships over material matters. Acknowledge the occasional small wager is acceptable, but explain that obsession over the next win and anxiety over a current loss is the sign of an emerging problem.

What makes gaming addictions so scary for parents is that problem gamblers can initially hide their betting behaviors quite skillfully. For a while, there are likely to be no outside signs that there is a problem: no needle marks, bloodshot eyes, or slurred speech, as with some other addictions. Furthermore, many teen gamers are strong students who are highly motivated to be successful. On the inside, however, these kids can't manage their impulsivity, and they often suffer from low self-esteem. When they lose, which they inevitably do, they lose control. Grades slip, household money goes missing, and relationships weaken. Many turn to additional addictions to mask their pain and frustration.

If you fear your teen is troubled and may have a problem with gambling, take a chance and have a supportive conversation that gets you closer to knowing what is really going on. If you find out your son does have a problem with compulsive gambling, understand that this is an addiction just as complex, and as potentially destructive, as addiction to alcohol or drugs. Don't try to go it alone. Get help. Contact a qualified therapist or counselor, or get free assistance 24 hours a day, seven days a week by visiting the web site for the National Problem Gaming Awareness Week at: http://www.npgaw.org/.

SPECIAL CHALLENGES:
Questions About Serious Teen Behavior Issues

---

39. DEALING WITH DEFIANT TEENS

Question: *My daughter, who just turned seventeen, has been breaking a lot of house rules ever since she got her driver's license. Some of the things she does feel like normal teenage behavior, but at other times her behavior feels excessive. How do I know when my daughter has crossed the line?*

THE PARENT PLAYBOOK

As teenagers enter the driving years, their behavior often changes. This is usually related to an adolescent's desire to develop her own identity and independence. Peers start to become more important than parents, and the ability to drive creates both newfound freedom and opportunity to push the boundaries of household rules. When gauging the seriousness of your rule-breaking teen's behavior consider the following warning signs. They will help you determine when your child has crossed the line and needs help.

- *Failure to respond to a verbal request in a reasonable amount of time.* What is "reasonable"? A minute or less! Yes, your child should respond to most requests almost instantly, especially simple ones like "Could you please call me if your plans change tonight?" Of course, you can't always expect your kids to do what you ask every single time, but they should acknowledge your comments and provide some type of acceptable response.

- *Consistent failure to keep doing what has been requested until the task has been finished.* When assigned a task, many teenagers don't follow through. They do the minimum, leave the job half finished, or take too long to respond, adding stress and anxiety to a parent's life. That's bound to happen from time to time. If, however, you have tactfully clarified expectations about what you expect, secured an agreement, and still find that your teen insists on under-performing, then the situation has become more serious.

- *Failure to follow through on well-understood rules.* Most parents have certain "ground rule" expectations of their offspring that don't, or at least shouldn't, need constant re-explanation: keep your room clean, go to school, be respectful to adults—that kind of thing. Kids get this. If your child is continually breaking these previously obeyed, well-understood rules at every turn, you both have a problem.

The point at which a teenager's troubles become serious varies from family to family, and ultimately it is your job as a parent to determine what is and isn't acceptable in your family. However, when you feel like you get no respite from the situation, your child has crossed the line and it is time to consult a professional.

40. DEALING WITH MENTAL HEALTH ISSUES

> **Question:** *How do I know whether my child has a mental health problem?*

This is difficult to determine without multiple therapy sessions. One factor complicating the situation is that the teen years are already quite complex when it comes to behavior. Even healthy kids may display alteration of mood, distressing thoughts, anxiety, impulsivity and other signs therapists associate with mental health concerns.

So how does a parent know when there is a genuine mental health problem? The best advice is to look at three factors: *frequency, intensity*, and *duration*.

Frequency is when something like anxiety or impulsive outbursts happen again and again. Occasional misbehaviors are actually developmentally appropriate; they're part of growing up. When the behavior crosses the line repeatedly and there is frequent parental worry, however, it is time to see a professional.

Duration is related to how long a specific incident takes. Does it last much longer than it should? For example, say your son received a poor grade. If it takes him weeks to get over it, you should be concerned. Most kids feel momentary frustration but then move on fairly quickly. If your child gets "stuck," it is time to see a professional.

Intensity is the "scare factor." How powerful was the behavior? Something happens—say, a peer breaks off a previously strong friendship—and your teen's reaction is so disproportionate that it creates tremendous worry for you. Of course, all kids make the occasional mistake in their relationships, and many pout, argue, or overreact in response to such problems. This is typical teen behavior. Some kids, however, react with extreme, overwhelming emotion: perhaps by hitting a wall; by making bitter, attacking, or otherwise inappropriately harsh comments; or by engaging in some kind of seemingly self-destructive behavior. Again, it is time to see a professional.

When determining the seriousness of your teen's behavior, look for evidence of any one of these three warning signals. Trust your gut, and don't hesitate to reach out for help to ensure your child is developmentally on track.

41. IS A WILDERNESS PROGRAM RIGHT FOR YOUR TEEN?

> **Question**: *Our daughter is really out of control. She has a drug problem. My husband and I are considering sending her to a wilderness program or a therapeutic boarding school, but we are hesitant. We know these are major steps we are considering, and we are afraid of how they might change our relationship with our daughter. At the same time, we feel we are out of options. How did all this happen . . . and what do we do now?*

These are difficult questions for any parent to ask, but you should know that you are not alone. Many families have faced this same concern; however, wilderness programs and therapeutic schools can change lives.

Questions About Compulsive Behaviors

Many children act out during their adolescent years; this is a normal part of the maturation process. However, when the turmoil is beyond the range of typical teen troubles (see Question 39), a major intervention is often needed. Students are sent to therapeutic programs for a variety of problems, including drinking, drugs, depression, bi-polar disorder, and any number of other challenges. There is, however, one common feature that underlies all of these issues: self-destructive behaviors that create crises.

As someone who has seen a lot of these cases, I can assure you that parents typically are not at fault when their teenagers misbehave or have behavioral issues. Unfortunately, many feel they are bad caregivers if they use a wilderness program. It is important to understand that there are multiple factors that contribute to the destructive downward spiral of teenage behavior. It's also important to recognize that a parent who realizes when a situation is beyond his or her control, and then takes appropriate action, is a good parent.

Most parents have experienced multiple failed interventions by the time they decide to enroll a teen in a program such as this. Typically, most have talked with multiple doctors, visited with a variety of therapists, and interacted with numerous school professionals. Unfortunately, nothing has worked. Some parents in this situation conclude, with good reason, that if they sit back and do nothing, their children will fail out of school and become unproductive members of society. I don't believe these people are "bad parents," but rather caring, engaged, loving caregivers acting in the best interests of their child.

The teenagers in this situation are not happy. On some level, they know they are struggling, but they often lack the maturity to reflect on the depth of their circumstances. They become angry and decide that it is easier to lose their thoughts in drugs, alcohol, and/or the computer, than it is to participate in a healthy, productive lifestyle. These kids have lost the ability to change. They need assistance if they are to transform themselves.

A residential environment may well be the best choice not only for your daughter, but for your family as a whole. This is, of course, a complicated decision, as there are hundreds of programs that offer a range of services, and a very small number of programs have received some bad press for a variety of reasons. To avoid any pitfalls and to ensure that you are using a reputable program with a quality therapeutic staff, I highly recommend working with an educational consultant. These professionals have extensive training and background with placing troubled teens. Consultants spend a significant amount of time on the road visiting schools and meeting with staff. They are extremely knowledgable individuals who will not only help you choose the best programs, but also guide and support your family through the entire process.

You can start on the path of locating the right educational consultant for your family by contacting me through my web site, www.ed-psy.com.

EPILOGUE:
Some Final Thoughts On Parenting

"We are apt to forget that children watch examples better than they listen to preaching."

- ROY L. SMITH

"To bring up a child in the way he should go, travel that way yourself once in a while."

- JOSH BILLINGS

"The best inheritance a parent can give his children is a few minutes of his time each day."

- O. A. BATTISTA

"If you want children to keep their feet on the ground, put some responsibility on their shoulders."

- ABIGAIL VAN BUREN

"Too often, we give children answers to remember rather than problems to solve."

- ROGER LEWIN

"Affirming words from moms and dads are like light switches. Speak a word of affirmation at the right moment in a child's life and it's like lighting up a whole roomful of possibilities."

- GARY SMALLEY

"If you want your children to improve, let them overhear the nice things you say about them to others."

- HAIM GINOTT

Some Final Thoughts On Parenting

"Feelings of worth can flourish only in an atmosphere where individual differences are appreciated, mistakes are tolerated, communication is open, and rules are flexible—the kind of atmosphere that is found in a nurturing family."

- VIRGINIA SATIR

"Parents need to fill a child's bucket of self-esteem so high that the rest of the world can't poke enough holes to drain it dry."

- ALVIN PRICE

"The guys who fear becoming fathers don't understand that fathering is not something perfect men do, but something that perfects the man. The end product of child-raising is not the child but the parent."

- FRANK PITTMAN

"You don't really understand human nature unless you know why a child on a merry-go-round will wave at his parents every time around - and why his parents will always wave back."

- WILLIAM D. TAMMEUS

"It would seem that something which means poverty, disorder, and violence every single day should be avoided entirely, but the desire to beget children is a natural urge."

- PHYLLIS DILLER

About the Author

Russell Hyken earned a Ph. D in Psychology from Capella University, an Educational Specialist degree from Webster University, a Masters of Arts in Counseling from Saint Louis University, teaching certi-fication from Washington University, and a B.A. in Communications and a B.S. in Marketing from Saint Louis University. With more than 15 years of experience in education as a teacher, school counselor, psychological examiner and school administrator, Hyken founded Educational and Psychotherapy Services, LLC in 2002. EPS specializes in residential placement assistance/interventions, educational evaluations, individual/family therapy and educational therapy.

Russell is a happily married father of two boys. He enjoys spending time with his family, running, and playing tennis. Russell feels strongly about working with and educating parents to help in the tumultuous child-rearing times. He writes articles for various family magazines and is often seen on regional TV news discussing how to have more discussions and fewer arguments with family members.